The Grill Sisters'
GUIDE TO
LEGENDARY
BBQ

The Grill Sisters'

GUIDE TO

LEGENDARY BBQ

60 Irresistible Recipes that Guarantee Mouthwatering, Finger-Lickin' Results

IRENE SHARP, Creator of Come Grill with Me **&**

DESI LONGINIDIS, Creator of Healthy Cook 4 Champions

Co-founders of The Grill Sisters

PAGE STREET
PUBLISHING CO.

PAGE STREET
PUBLISHING CO.

First published in 2023 by
Page Street Publishing Co.
27 Congress Street, Suite 1511
Salem, MA 01970
www.pagestreetpublishing.com

Distributed by Macmillan, sales in Canada by The Canadian Manda Group.

27 26 25 24 23   1 2 3 4 5

ISBN-13: 978-1-64567-980-6
ISBN-10: 1-64567-980-2

Library of Congress Control Number: 2022935238

Cover and book design by Emma Hardy for Page Street Publishing Co.
Photography and styling by Irene Sharp and Desi Longinidis

Printed and bound in China

DEDICATION

TO OUR CHILDREN:
Susannah, Isaac and Jackson

TABLE OF *Contents*

INTRODUCTION

We believe grilling is an outdoor celebration that brings family and friends together, one with the power to ignite a creative passion for unforgettable food. For us, the key to amazing barbecue has always been using the best grilling methods and techniques, as well as using the freshest ingredients available.

Our motivation for writing this book and sharing our recipes is the hope that you, too, will find a passion for barbecue. You'll learn about many exciting cooking methods such as skillet cooking, searing, reverse searing, pan basting and smoking, as well as about the Maillard reaction and direct and indirect cooking. Whether you're cooking on a gas grill, charcoal kettle, offset smoker or pellet grill, we'll show you that cooking outdoors can be fun, easy and, without a doubt, legendary. Be prepared to grill the perfect steak, enjoy irresistible food and tantalizing aromas, as well as explore flavors that are beyond any you've ever experienced before.

Over the years, we've been blessed with an incredible social media following and we regularly share our grilling journey with the world. Desi is the founder of Healthy Cook 4 Champions and Irene is the founder of Come Grill With Me—and together, we're "the Grill Sisters." We've worked with many grilling brands around the world and we're ambassadors of Australia's largest barbecue store, Barbeques Galore.

We've appeared on Australian television and showcased our skills on Australia's best barbecue television show, Channel 7's *7Mate Dipper's Backyard BBQ Wars*, and hosted the World Food Championships Australia. We share the art of grilling at every opportunity we get. On a daily basis, we get asked lots of questions regarding the methods we use and the recipes we love creating and eating. We're thrilled to be able to include them all in this book.

Since we both lead busy lives as working mothers and wives, cooking delicious food outdoors with fire is how we unwind and connect with nature. This book is a collection of the meals our family and friends love. The recipes we've included have been created, cooked and perfected over years—some we've been cooking since we were teenagers (we both grilled our first octopus at 10 years of age, and we cooked the perfect steak at 12 years of age). Some of these recipes were inspired by the countries we've travelled to and the grilling methods and techniques we've spent years mastering.

We had many catch-ups to talk about the recipes we'd include in our book. We often got side-tracked by childhood memories when we discussed old family favorite recipes that have stood the test of time, and that we put our own spin on to cook using a grill. Yes, we've included those, too.

Feeding people is in our blood and it virtually started the moment we could walk and talk. Growing up, our beautiful mother Virginia worked three jobs to support us and our two younger sisters all on her own. She encouraged us at an early age to be creative in the kitchen and we often cooked up a storm, with what little we had back then. As teenagers, we discovered the art of barbecue and how special the char-grilled flavor of food can be. We could only afford a disposable $13 foil tray that came with charcoal, but it did the job. What mattered to us was that we were outdoors cooking. Fast forward to our adult lives: we own more grills than most people, we're married to amazing husbands and we have adorable children who all love the food we cook for them.

Today, grilling anchors a large part of our lives and we wanted to ensure there's something for everyone and every occasion in our cookbook, from traditional barbecue favorites like burgers and ribs to exotic grilled meals using seafood, meat, poultry and vegetables. We have even included a chapter with the most indulgent desserts cooked outdoors—or, if you must, indoors.

Finally, we hope you enjoy our barbecue recipes and techniques as much as we have absolutely loved bringing them together in our very own cookbook. This book is a dream come true for both of us and we've put our hearts and souls into every page. Enjoy your barbecue journey. We are so glad you have joined us.

Love,
Irene Sharp and Desi Longinidis

GRILLING 101

In this section, we've included some of the questions we get asked the most about charcoal grilling, direct and indirect grilling, internal temperatures and how to pair smoking woods with meat, seafood and vegetables. Keep this information on hand to bring your grilling skills to the next level.

FREQUENTLY ASKED GRILLING QUESTIONS

HOW DO YOU LIGHT A CHARCOAL GRILL?

Getting a charcoal grill started can seem daunting. We're often asked for our tips on lighting a charcoal grill, so here they are:

- Use a mix of lump natural hardwood charcoal and briquettes. Lump charcoal will light faster and the briquettes will last longer. We use the same weight of charcoal as that of the meat we're cooking or smoking.

- Buy the largest charcoal chimney starter you can find. You can have charcoal ready in 15 to 20 minutes using a chimney.

- Fill a charcoal chimney with lump and briquettes and place it on the fire grate, then add four natural firelighters underneath.

Charcoal chimney

Briquettes (left and bottom right) and lump charcoal (top right)

WHAT'S THE DIFFERENCE BETWEEN DIRECT AND INDIRECT BBQ GRILLING?

Direct grilling is when food is placed directly on top of a grill grate, over high heat. This method is perfect for thinner and smaller pieces of meat such as burgers, steaks, chicken, pork, seafood and some vegetables. When using the direct grilling method, the temperature you would use ranges from medium 350 to 450°F (175 to 230°C) and high 450 to 550°F (230 to 290°C).

Indirect grilling cooks food slowly and with lower heat, and is great for imparting a smoky flavor. Food is never placed directly over high heat but instead sits opposite the heat source. Indirect cooking is ideal for thicker and larger pieces of meat such as fall-off-the-bone roasts, ribs, whole chickens and most BBQ desserts. When using the indirect grilling method, the temperature you would use ranges from 250 to 350°F (120 to 175°C).

HOW DO YOU SET UP A CHARCOAL GRILL FOR INDIRECT COOKING?

When you're cooking with charcoal, pour the lit charcoal on one half of the fire grate. Place your meat on the grill grate side that doesn't have charcoal lit underneath. For low and slow cooking, it's best to place an aluminium tray (or a drip pan) filled with water or stock on the bottom cooking grate in your barbecue, directly under the meat you are cooking, to keep it moist.

HOW DO YOU SET UP A GAS GRILL FOR INDIRECT COOKING?

An important start to cooking with gas is ensuring your gas propane tank is full. We always keep a spare tank so we never run out midway through a cook. For indirect cooking on a gas grill, set the outer burners to low to medium heat and leave the center burner off. Place your meat over the area that isn't lit. If you're using a two-burner gas grill, turn one side off and set the other to low.

Direct cooking with charcoal

Direct cooking with gas

Indirect cooking with charcoal

Indirect cooking with gas

SMOKING WOOD

When using wood chips, we like to soak them in apple juice or a 50 percent water/50 percent apple cider mix. If they're not soaked prior to being added directly to charcoal or in a smoke box, they're more likely to burn. When using chunks of smoking wood, we add them directly to charcoal that's lit and ready to be used.

SMOKING WOOD	FLAVOR	USE WITH
Apple	Fruity, sweet, mild	Beef, lamb, poultry, seafood, veggies
Maple	Sweet, mild	Poultry, seafood, veggies
Cherry	Sweet, mild	Beef, lamb, pork, poultry, seafood
Peach	Sweet, mild	Pork, poultry, seafood, veggies
Oak	Mild	Beef, lamb, pork, poultry
Hickory	Strong, bold, with a hint of bacon flavor	Beef, pork, poultry
Pecan	Sweet, nutty, rich in flavor	Beef, pork, poultry
Mesquite	Strong, smoky, spicy	Beef, lamb, pork, poultry
Walnut	Can be bitter, best paired with another wood	Beef, pork
Alder	Light, sweet, woody flavor	Beef, lamb, pork, poultry, seafood
Pear	Light, sweet	Pork, poultry, veggies
Citrus	Light, mild	Lamb, seafood, veggies
Plum	Sweet, mild	Pork, poultry, seafood
Orange	Mild, tangy, hint of fruitiness	Beef, pork, poultry, veggies

MINIMUM INTERNAL TEMPERATURE GUIDE

This is a quick reference guide that will take the guesswork out of grilling all your meats and seafoods to a minimum safe-to-eat temperature.

Beef roast	145°F (65°C)
Ground beef	160°F (70°C)
Lamb—chops, loin, roast	145°F (65°C)
Pork—chops, ham, roast	145°F (65°C)
Poultry—chicken, turkey, duck	165°F (75°C)
Veal—chops	145°F (65°C)
Fish & shellfish—fillets, salmon, crab, lobster	145°F (65°C)
Shrimp, scallops	Cook until opaque
Clams, oysters, mussels	Cook until they open

STEAK INTERNAL TEMPERATURE GUIDE

This is a quick reference guide to cooking steak to your preferred doneness.

Rare	120–125°F (49–50°C)
Medium rare	125–135°F (50–60°C)
Medium	135–145°F (60–65°C)
Medium well	145–155°F (65–68°C)
Well done	155–165°F (68–75°C)

Best Ever
BEEF & LAMB

Our hearty beef and lamb barbecue meals have always been popular with our families and friends. Once we began sharing them online, we quickly discovered how much everyone else loved them, too!

We love combining delicious herbs and spices in our marinades and creating new seasonings that complement the beef and lamb cuts we grill.

In this chapter, we share our popular recipes for steaks, roasts, koftas, burgers, tacos, souvlaki, ribs and cutlets. A few of our favorites are the Ridiculously Good Chili Espresso Ribeye (page 16) that is cooked over direct heat, the Moroccan Lamb Rack with Red Wine Pomegranate Sauce (page 48), which uses the indirect method, or the Beef Short Ribs with Bourbon BBQ Sauce (page 41) for the longer low and slow cook. We also share with you the methods and techniques that help achieve barbecue magic. So, grab your tongs and let's get grilling!

Ridiculously Good
CHILI ESPRESSO RIBEYE

YIELD
4 servings

Over the years, we have experimented with different seasonings to create rubs that impart delicious flavors to the proteins we grill. One sunny afternoon, while having a sister catch-up over an espresso, we entertained the idea of adding our favorite ground coffee to our next rub creation. As ridiculous as it sounded at the time, it worked and was so good that our friends and family couldn't get enough of it to use on their steaks. This espresso and chili rub is earthy, delicious and addictive! The coffee not only acts as a tenderizer but also provides an incredible crust on steaks, while the chili powder adds an unforgettable spicy kick. This is a must-have steak rub to keep in the pantry.

CHILI ESPRESSO RUB

2 tbsp (36 g) kosher salt

1 tsp ground cumin

2 tbsp (14 g) coffee, finely ground

2 tbsp (16 g) ground chili powder

1 tsp ground sweet paprika

½ tsp ground mustard powder

1 tsp garlic powder

1 tsp ground black pepper

RIBEYE

2 (1-lb [454-g]) ribeye steaks

2 tbsp (30 ml) extra virgin olive oil

Baked potato and butter, for serving

Steamed green beans, for serving

To make the Chili Espresso Rub, mix the salt, cumin, coffee, chili powder, paprika, mustard powder, garlic powder and black pepper in a small bowl until well combined.

Coat the ribeye steaks with olive oil and then apply the chili espresso coffee rub equally to each. Use one hand to sprinkle the rub onto the steaks and the other to massage it into the meat. Then cover the steaks with cling wrap and allow them to reach room temperature (this will take approximately 30 minutes). When the steaks are at room temperature prior to grilling, they're more likely to cook evenly.

Ten minutes prior to grilling your steaks, prepare a gas grill for direct heat using a grill grate and preheat it to 390°F (200°C). When the grill is ready, cook the seasoned steaks over direct heat for 5 to 6 minutes a side for a medium-rare doneness or until the internal temperature reaches 135°F (60°C). If you prefer your ribeye steaks with a medium doneness, cook them for 6 to 8 minutes a side or until the internal temperature reaches 145°F (65°C).

Transfer the steaks to a tray or roasting tin, cover loosely with aluminium foil and let them rest for 5 to 10 minutes. Slice the steaks and serve with a baked potato with lots of butter and green beans.

 NOTE: The Chili Espresso Rub can be stored in a Mason jar for 4 to 6 months, so make extra to save time with your next cook.

FLAME-GRILLED FILET *with* MUSHROOM WINE SAUCE

YIELD
4 servings

This is a superb recipe for those nights when you want a restaurant-quality meal in the comfort of your home, fabulously fast! We use beef tenderloin for this recipe; it is incredibly tender and tasty when cooked hot and fast on a grill grate over fire. The steak is paired with a delicious full-bodied mushroom red wine sauce that is easy to make, yet impressive when spooned over the flame-kissed filet mignon. The sauce complements most beef cuts but we feel that the filet mignon is perfect for this recipe.

FILET MIGNON

4 (6-oz [170-g]) filet mignon steaks

1 tbsp (15 ml) olive oil

Salt

Black pepper

MUSHROOM WINE SAUCE

2 tbsp (30 ml) oil

1 small yellow onion, chopped

Salt and pepper, to taste

7 oz (200 g) fresh white mushrooms, thinly sliced

2 cloves garlic, crushed

1 tbsp (14 g) all-purpose flour

1 cup (240 ml) full-bodied red wine, such as Merlot

2 tbsp (28 g) butter

Steamed snow peas, for serving

Coat the steaks with the olive oil and season with salt and pepper. Allow the steaks to reach room temperature.

Prepare a gas grill for direct heat using a grill grate and preheat it to 390°F (200°C). Grill the steaks, with the lid up, for 8 to 10 minutes for medium-rare doneness or until the internal temperature reaches 135°F (60°C). For medium doneness, grill the steaks for 10 to 12 minutes or until the internal temperature reaches 145°F (65°C). Remove the steaks from the grill and rest them, loosely covered with aluminium foil, while you make the sauce.

To make the mushroom red wine sauce, reduce the grill's heat to medium-low. To a small saucepan, add the oil, onion, salt and pepper and sauté for 5 minutes, until the onion is softened and golden. Add the mushrooms and garlic and cook for an additional 5 minutes, stirring occasionally.

Add the flour and cook for 1 minute, constantly stirring. Then add the wine and butter and gently simmer, stirring occasionally for 10 minutes. Remove the sauce from the heat when there are no lumps and it has slightly thickened.

Spoon the mushroom sauce over the steaks and serve with steamed snow peas.

SKILLET SURF & TURF *with* VODKA GARLIC BUTTER

This meal combines the best of both worlds. There's a tender, juicy steak served with plump vodka and garlic-infused buttery shrimp that will surely impress guests at your dinner table.

In this recipe, we use a kettle grill with the lid open for direct hot and fast charcoal grilling and a cooking method called the Maillard reaction. This method is responsible for the flavor-packed crusts you see in steak restaurants and is easy to achieve at home. When using this method, we like to ensure that beef is brought to room temperature, that it is seasoned well with salt and that we're using a cast-iron skillet, which can withstand the heat required for the Maillard reaction to create its magic.

We use fresh shrimp in this recipe but thawed frozen shrimp will be just as delicious. The homemade vodka garlic butter and fresh parsley provide a divine boost of flavor to this surf and turf dish without being overpowering.

SURF AND TURF

1 (1-lb [454-g]) T-bone steak

1 tbsp (18 g) kosher salt

2 tbsp (30 ml) extra virgin olive oil

14–16 large, peeled and deveined fresh shrimp with the tails on (or frozen and thawed)

Crisp green beans, for serving

VODKA GARLIC BUTTER

7 tbsp (100 g) unsalted butter, softened

½ tsp kosher salt

½ tbsp (4 g) chopped fresh parsley

2 cloves garlic, crushed

3 tbsp (45 ml) vodka

To draw out moisture in the steak, pat it with paper towels and season it with the salt. Then bring the steak to room temperature (this will take approximately 30 minutes).

Meanwhile, make the Vodka Garlic Butter. Place the softened butter, kosher salt, fresh parsley, crushed garlic and vodka in a small bowl and whisk until they're well combined. Then transfer the butter mixture onto a sheet of cling wrap and shape it into a log, twisting the ends of the plastic to seal it. Place the butter in the freezer for at least 30 minutes before using it.

Prepare a charcoal grill for direct heat, and preheat it to 375°F (190°C). Grease a cast-iron skillet with the oil and place it on the grill directly over the charcoal for 1 to 2 minutes, leaving the lid off the grill.

When the skillet is hot, achieve a Maillard reaction by searing the steak in the skillet for 3 minutes on each side for medium-rare doneness or until the steak reaches an internal temperature of 135°F (60°C). For medium doneness, cook the steak for 4 to 5 minutes per side, or until it reaches an internal temperature of 145°F (65°C). Remove the steak from the skillet and tent it with foil for 5 minutes.

(continued)

Meanwhile, cut two 2-inch (5-cm) slices of the Vodka Garlic Butter and add them to the hot skillet. As the butter melts, add the shrimp and cook for 2 to 3 minutes on each side. You'll know they're ready when they turn completely opaque. Return the steak to the skillet for 1 minute to heat through and gently baste with the remaining melted Vodka Garlic Butter in the skillet.

Remove the steak and shrimp from the skillet. Then slice the steak thinly against the grain and divide it between two serving plates topped with the shrimp and a side of crisp green beans. Drizzle the skillet juices over the steak and shrimp to serve.

 NOTE: You can store any leftover butter in the freezer for up to 6 months wrapped in cling wrap or parchment paper.

MEDITERRANEAN KOFTAS *with* GARLIC SAUCE & TOMATO SALSA

YIELD
4 servings
(3 koftas
per serving)

This is our take on one of our family's secret recipes. The original recipe has dried herbs and no sauces, but here, we have added fresh mint and parsley, Worcestershire sauce and ketchup to create big, bold flavors in every bite. The meat mixture makes 12 perfect-sized koftas that will cook through evenly. Make sure you have twelve metal skewers ready as you will need one per kofta. The koftas will need to sit in the fridge for at least 30 minutes and up to overnight so all the flavors can infuse into the meat. These koftas combined with the garlic sauce and tomato salsa are so delicious and can be eaten as a meze or main course.

KOFTAS

1 lb (454 g) ground beef

1 red onion, finely diced

3 cloves garlic, crushed

1 egg

½ cup (60 g) breadcrumbs

1 cup (60 g) chopped fresh parsley

½ cup (46 g) chopped fresh mint

1 tbsp (7 g) ground sweet paprika

1½ tsp (9 g) sea salt

½ tsp cracked pepper

2 tbsp (11 g) dried mint

1 tbsp (15 ml) ketchup

2 tbsp (30 ml) Worcestershire sauce

1 tbsp (7 g) chili flakes (optional)

3 tbsp (45 ml) olive oil, divided

4 pita breads

8 lettuce leaves, shredded, for serving

1 lemon, cut into wedges

GARLIC SAUCE

¾ cup (180 ml) Greek yogurt

4 cloves garlic, minced

2 tbsp (30 ml) fresh lemon juice

Salt, to taste

To make the Koftas, in a medium bowl, mix the beef, onion, garlic, egg, breadcrumbs, fresh parsley and mint, sweet paprika, salt, pepper, dried mint, ketchup, Worcestershire sauce and chili flakes (if using).

Use damp hands to make it easier to divide and shape the meat mixture into twelve equal portions. Using both hands, roll each portion into sausage shapes, then thread the skewer through the middle of the portion and place the finished skewers on a plate. Cover the finished skewers with cling wrap and leave them in the refrigerator for at least 30 minutes or overnight for the flavors to infuse into the meat.

To make the Garlic Sauce, in a small bowl, gently stir together the yogurt, garlic, lemon juice and salt until just combined. If you over stir the yogurt sauce, it will become too runny. Pour the mixture into a container and refrigerate until needed. The sauce can be made a few days in advance, to save time.

(continued)

MEDITERRANEAN KOFTAS *with*
GARLIC SAUCE & TOMATO SALSA *(continued)*

TOMATO SALSA

1 cup (149 g) diced mixed cherry tomatoes

½ cup (66 g) diced cucumber

½ red onion, finely diced

2 tbsp (30 ml) extra virgin olive oil

2 tbsp (30 ml) lemon juice

Salt and pepper, to taste

To make the Tomato Salsa, mix the tomatoes, cucumber, onion, olive oil, lemon juice, salt and pepper in a small bowl. Set it aside until needed.

Prepare a gas grill for direct grilling using a hotplate and preheat it to 390°F (200°C). Set the grill to medium-high heat 10 minutes prior to cooking. Lightly grease the preheated hotplate with 2 tablespoons (30 ml) of the olive oil and cook the Koftas for approximately 8 minutes total, turning frequently. When the Koftas are slightly browned in the middle, they're cooked.

Prepare for serving by brushing the remaining 1 tablespoon (15 ml) of olive oil on both sides of each pita bread. Place each pita over the preheated grill grate side of the grill and grill for approximately 30 seconds per side, then remove them from the heat.

Serve the Koftas on the slightly grilled pita bread with the lettuce, Garlic Sauce, Tomato Salsa and lemon wedges for squeezing.

 NOTE: If you're using wooden skewers, soak them for 30 minutes before threading the kofta mixture so they don't burn during the cooking process.

BEER & GARLIC PEPPERED STEAKS *with* TWICE-COOKED FRIES

YIELD
4 servings

A big, juicy and tasty steak is what every cook aspires to achieve. We're always experimenting with different methods, brines and marinades to find ways to do this. Beer is one of our favorite ingredients to add! Beer in a marinade imparts flavor to steaks while helping retain natural juices. The longer you leave this marinade to work its magic, the tastier and more tender the result. In this recipe, we've paired the ever-popular New York strip (called Porterhouse in Australia) steak with crisp, fluffy and golden twice-cooked fries. We like to use a grill grate to cook the steaks and the gas side burner to cook the potatoes.

STEAK

1 cup (240 ml) brown ale or stout beer

3 cloves garlic, crushed

3 tbsp (45 ml) Worcestershire sauce

2 tbsp (30 ml) olive oil

1 tsp ground mustard powder

2 tsp (10 ml) Dijon mustard

1 tbsp (6 g) cracked pepper

2 tsp (12 g) salt

4 (6-oz [170-g]) New York strip steaks

FRIES

½ lb (226 g) russet potatoes, peeled and cut into ½-inch (1-cm) fries

Light olive oil or vegetable oil, for deep frying

Kosher salt to season

To make the marinade, in a bowl whisk together the beer, garlic, Worcestershire sauce, olive oil, mustard powder, Dijon mustard, pepper and salt. Place the steaks in a dish and pour half the marinade on top of the steaks. Then flip the steaks over and pour the remaining marinade mixture on them. Cover the steaks with cling wrap and leave them in the fridge to marinate for at least 4 hours or overnight.

Before cooking, remove the steaks from the marinade and allow them to reach room temperature. Reserve the marinade to use for basting the steaks when they're on the grill.

Soak the potatoes in cold water for 5 minutes. Drain them and pat dry with paper towels. Place the potatoes in a large saucepan and cover them with cold water. Using a gas side burner or directly on a grill grate, over medium-high heat, simmer the potatoes for about 5 minutes or until they are par cooked. When the potatoes are par cooked, drain them and rinse under cold water. This will stop the cooking process. Then pat them dry with paper towels to remove the moisture. Set them aside to dry until needed. They need to be as dry as possible to get them crispy when they're frying in the oil.

Prepare a grill for direct grilling with the lid open and preheat it to 390°F (200°C). Brush the steaks with the remaining marinade throughout the cook, being mindful of potential flare-ups due to the beer in the marinade.

(continued)

Grill the steaks for 3 to 4 minutes per side to achieve a medium-rare doneness or until an internal temperature of 135°F (60°C) is reached. For medium doneness, cook the steak for 4 to 5 minutes per side or until an internal temperature of 145°F (65°C) is achieved. When cooked to your preference, set the steaks aside to rest for 5 minutes.

As the steaks are resting, fry the potatoes. Add enough oil to cover the potatoes to a large pot and heat it to 350°F (175°C) using the side gas burner. Cook two to three handfuls of potatoes per batch in the oil. Cook for about 3 minutes per batch or until the potatoes are golden in color. When all the potatoes are cooked, season them with salt and serve with the steak.

THE DELUXE BURGER—*With the Lot!*

YIELD
4 servings

Growing up in Australia, ordering a big burger with the lot from the local fish 'n' chips shop was a Friday night must! When a burger has "the lot," it's loaded with cheese, bacon, egg, lettuce, tomato, beets and ketchup. Fast forward to adult life, our burger with the lot not only brings back great childhood memories but leaves even the hungriest guest totally satisfied. We use our tried-and-true beef patty recipe, passed down from our mother, that we've tweaked a little. Roll up your sleeves and get your appetite ready, because things are about to get drool-worthy messy!

BEEF PATTIES
1 lb (454 g) ground beef, 70/30 fat ratio

1 small yellow onion, diced

2 cloves garlic, crushed

¼ cup (23 g) chopped fresh mint

¼ cup (15 g) chopped fresh parsley

2 tbsp (11 g) dried mint

1 tbsp (15 ml) ketchup

2 tbsp (30 ml) Worcestershire sauce

1 egg

½ cup (60 g) breadcrumbs

1 tsp salt

½ tsp pepper

Olive oil, for grilling

BURGER SAUCE
1 cup (240 ml) mayonnaise

2 tbsp (30 ml) yellow mustard

1 tbsp (15 ml) ketchup

1 tbsp (9 g) finely chopped whole dill pickles

1 tsp onion powder

1 tsp garlic powder

1 tsp Dijon mustard

ONIONS
4 large Spanish onions, sliced

2 tbsp (28 g) unsalted butter

½ tsp salt

To make the patties, place the ground beef, onion, garlic, fresh mint, parsley, dried mint, ketchup, Worcestershire sauce, egg, breadcrumbs, salt and pepper in a large bowl and combine well using your hands. Divide the mixture into four equal portions and shape them into round burger patties. Refrigerate the burger patties until needed.

To make the Burger Sauce, mix the mayonnaise, yellow mustard, ketchup, pickles, onion powder, garlic powder and Dijon mustard. Refrigerate the sauce until needed.

Prepare a grill for direct grilling, using a grill grate and a hotplate, and preheat it to 390°F (200°C).

To prepare the onions, place the onions, butter and salt on the hotplate all at the same time and cook for 4 to 5 minutes or until softened. Use metal tongs to turn the onions midway through the cooking time. Remove them from the hotplate when cooked and place them in a bowl covered with aluminium foil to keep them warm.

Brush the beef patties with oil and grill them on the hotplate for 4 minutes per side or until cooked through. Place a slice of cheese on each burger patty in the last minute so it melts.

On the hotplate, cook the bacon strips for approximately 2 to 3 minutes on each side, or until they're cooked to your liking. Remove the bacon from the heat.

Crack the eggs onto the hotplate and cook them sunny side–up (until the whites are set but the yolk is still runny) in the residual bacon fat. The bacon fat will add more flavor to the egg.

(continued)

THE DELUXE BURGER—*With the Lot! (continued)*

TO SERVE

4 slices American cheese, Colby or Swiss cheese (any easy-melt cheese works)

8 strips bacon

4 eggs

4 burger buns

Olive oil, for brushing

Lettuce leaves

8 tomato slices

8 slices canned beets

¼ cup (60 ml) ketchup

Brush the inside of the burger buns with oil and cook them on the grill grate for 2 to 3 seconds a side, to slightly toast.

To serve, spread 1 teaspoon of the Burger Sauce on the top and base of the buns. Top the base with lettuce, tomato, onion, beet slices, the burger patty, bacon, ketchup and the egg.

GREEK LAMB ROAST *with* LEMONY POTATOES

YIELD
6–8
servings

As children, we would always look forward to our mother's Sunday roast. We could always smell the incredible flavors throughout the whole house and even in our street. This is our version of our mother's classic dish, with a side of citrusy roast potatoes. Be prepared for an abundance of delicious aromas in your backyard as the lamb roast cooks. You'll also need to allow a 4-hour cook time, which will reward you with a scrumptious fall-off-the-bone roast.

MARINADE
¼ cup (60 ml) olive oil

1 tbsp (3 g) dried oregano

1 tbsp (7 g) sweet paprika

1 tbsp (7 g) onion powder

1 tbsp (18 g) sea salt

½ tsp pepper

2 cloves garlic, crushed

LEG OF LAMB AND LEMONY POTATOES
4.8 lb (2.2 k) leg of lamb, bone in

10 cloves garlic, peeled

1 tbsp (18 g) sea salt

2 tbsp (3 g) fresh rosemary sprigs

1 tbsp (15 ml) olive oil

2 large red onions, peeled (1 sliced ½ inch [1 cm] thick, 1 sliced into wedges)

2 cups (480 ml) chicken stock

1 large lemon, juiced

6 russet potatoes, peeled and cut into wedges

1 tsp dried oregano

8 sprigs dried thyme, plus more for serving

Lemon wedges, for serving

To make the marinade, in a small bowl, mix the olive oil, oregano, sweet paprika, onion powder, salt, pepper and garlic.

Remove any excess fat from the leg of lamb. Using a small sharp knife, cut seven slits on the top and three slits on the bottom of the leg of lamb deep enough for a clove of garlic to fit in, approximately ¾ inch (2 cm) deep. Push a clove of garlic into each slit. Sprinkle the salt all over the lamb and rub into the meat.

Place the lamb in a deep dish and pour the marinade all over the leg of the lamb, top and bottom. Cover with cling wrap. Refrigerate for 4 hours or preferably overnight.

When you're ready to begin cooking, remove the leg of lamb from the refrigerator and allow it to rest at room temperature for 30 minutes. As the leg of lamb is resting, insert a small sprig of rosemary into each slit that has the garlic, on the top of the lamb.

Set a gas barbecue for indirect cooking (see the Frequently Asked Grilling Questions section on page 10) and preheat it to 320°F (160°C) with the hood down.

Grease a roasting pan with the olive oil. Place the onion slices in the middle of the greased roasting pan then place the leg of lamb on top of the sliced onion. Add 1 cup (240 ml) of the chicken stock and half of the lemon juice to the pan. Cover the pan tightly with foil and place it on the grill on the side opposite the flame. Cook for 2½ hours, basting the leg of lamb with its own juices every 20 minutes, always re-covering the pan with the foil after bastings.

(continued)

After 2½ hours, add the potatoes, the remaining 1 cup (240 ml) of chicken stock and remaining lemon juice, and arrange the oregano and thyme sprigs around the leg of lamb. Cover again with foil.

Cook for 1 additional hour with the foil on, then remove the foil and cook for an additional 30 minutes. The leg of lamb should feel soft to touch and the potatoes should be crunchy on the outside and soft on the inside.

Arrange the potatoes around the leg of lamb on a platter with some fresh thyme sprigs and lemon wedges.

GRILLED LAMB SOUVLAKI *with* FRIES, SALAD & HOMEMADE TZATZIKI

YIELD
4 servings

Our Greek heritage and our beautiful mother should take credit for our ability to prepare this delicious fast food known as the humble lamb souvlaki. Traditionally, in Greece, a souvlaki includes tender pork, homemade tzatziki, salad and hot fries. While you can substitute the lamb in our recipe for pork or chicken, we think we've mastered the flavor combos in our souvlaki. Stuffing it with hot fries takes it to a whole new foodie heaven level!

SOUVLAKI

¼ cup (60 ml) olive oil

3 cloves garlic, crushed

2 tsp (2 g) dried oregano

1 tsp dried thyme

½ lemon, juiced

½ tsp salt

½ tsp pepper

1 lb (454 g) lamb loins (backstrap)

1 red bell pepper, sliced

1 green bell pepper, sliced

2 tbsp (30 ml) olive oil, for brushing

1 small Spanish onion, thinly sliced

4 large flatbread (pita) breads

TZATZIKI

½ cup (65 g) grated cucumber

1 cup (240 ml) Greek yogurt

2 cloves garlic, grated

1 tbsp (3 g) fresh dill, finely chopped

2 tbsp (11 g) fresh mint, finely chopped

1 tbsp (15 ml) lemon juice

¼ tsp salt

1 tbsp (15 ml) olive oil

To make the marinade, in a medium bowl, whisk the olive oil, garlic, oregano, thyme, lemon juice, salt and pepper until well combined. Set aside.

Cut the lamb loins in half lengthwise and then into 2-inch (5-cm) cubes. Add the lamb to the bowl with the marinade and coat it well. Marinate for at least 20 minutes. Then thread the lamb cubes on metal skewers.

While the lamb marinates, make the Tzatziki. Because cucumbers release liquid and can make the tzatziki runny, add the grated cucumber to a sieve and use a spoon to press out as much liquid as possible. Add the pressed cucumber to a small bowl with the Greek yogurt, garlic, dill, mint, lemon juice, salt and olive oil and stir to mix. Refrigerate until needed.

Prepare a gas grill for direct cooking, with a grate on one side and a hotplate on the other, and preheat it to 390°F (200°C). Cook the lamb skewers on the grill grate for 8 to 10 minutes, turning frequently for a medium doneness. Remove the lamb skewers from the grill, cover them loosely with foil and let them rest for 2 to 5 minutes.

While the lamb rests, brush the skin side of the bell peppers with the olive oil. Cook the bell peppers, skin-side down, along with the onions, on the hotplate for about 8 minutes, or until soft. Remove them from the hotplate and keep them warm in a small bowl, covered with aluminium foil.

(continued)

FRIES

½ lb (226 g) russet potatoes, peeled and cut into ½-inch (1-cm) slices

Light olive oil or vegetable oil, for deep frying

Kosher salt to season

FOR SERVING

2 cups (40 g) mixed lettuce leaves

1 tomato, diced

1 medium cucumber, sliced

To make the fries, use the side burner of a gas grill and add the oil to a large pot. Preheat the oil to 350°F (175°C). Cook two to three handfuls of fries per batch in the oil for 3 to 4 minutes or until they're golden in color. Season the fries with the salt.

Cook the flatbreads (pita) for 30 seconds each over medium, direct heat and place them on a plate.

To serve, in a medium bowl, toss the lettuce leaves, tomatoes and cucumbers to make a salad. Then assemble the souvlaki by adding a spoonful of tzatziki, some salad, fries, peppers, onions and one lamb skewer to each flatbread.

CARNE ASADA BEEF TACOS *with* CHARRED CORN & TOMATO SALSA

YIELD
8 servings

Carne asada means grilled marinated meat and we've created these carne asada beef tacos packed full of flavor, using a recipe we've cooked for our families for years. Everything can be prepared ahead of time and the beef is cooked over fire outdoors within minutes, which makes these perfect for a hectic weeknight or laid-back weekend. We love gathering around the dinner table and watching our family build their own tacos and devouring them.

STEAK

2 tbsp (30 ml) olive oil

¼ cup (60 ml) fresh lime juice

¼ cup (60 ml) red wine vinegar

1 tsp ground cumin

1 tsp sugar

1 tsp onion powder

4 cloves garlic, crushed

1 tsp salt

½ tsp pepper

1.3 lb (600 g) beef skirt steak

CHARRED CORN AND TOMATO SALSA

3 ears sweet corn, husks removed

2 tbsp (30 ml) avocado oil, divided

7 oz (200 g) cherry tomatoes

1 tbsp (7 g) diced red onion

¼ cup (4 g) cilantro

1 fresh lime, juiced

1 tsp salt

FOR SERVING

8 small corn tortillas

Sour cream

To marinate the steak, in a medium bowl, whisk the olive oil, lime juice, red wine vinegar, cumin, sugar, onion powder, garlic, salt and pepper until well combined. Place the steak in a ziptop bag and pour the marinade into the bag. Marinate for at least 2 hours or overnight, if possible. The marinade helps tenderize the skirt steak and adds flavor.

To make the Charred Corn and Tomato Salsa, coat each ear of corn with 1 teaspoon of the avocado oil. Preheat a grill to medium heat. Cook the corn over direct heat using a grill grate for 6 minutes, turning frequently, until the corn is slightly charred. Let the corn cool, then remove the kernels from the corn cobs and place them in a medium bowl.

Chop the tomatoes in half and place them along with the diced onion in the bowl with the charred corn kernels. Add the cilantro, lime juice, remaining 1 tablespoon (15 ml) of avocado oil and salt, then stir all the ingredients until well combined. Refrigerate until needed.

Prepare a grill for direct grilling, using a grill grate, and preheat it to 390°F (200°C).

Grill the skirt steak over direct high heat on a grill grate for 4 to 5 minutes a side for medium doneness. Rest the steak for 5 minutes, to allow the juices to redistribute into the beef. Then slice against the grain into strips.

While the steak rests, grill the tortillas, turning frequently over high heat for 10 seconds or until you see grill marks.

To serve, add a portion of grilled skirt steak, Charred Corn and Tomato Salsa and sour cream to each tortilla.

BEEF SHORT RIBS *with* BOURBON BBQ SAUCE

YIELD
8 servings

An important ingredient for the best beef short ribs is your time! We recommend allowing at least 7 hours cook time for these ribs and let us assure you, it will be worth the wait. When cooking beef ribs, we like to use a Traeger® grill, but feel free to use your smoker or charcoal kettle of choice. We've cooked plenty of tender beef ribs over the years and while buying quality beef is important, so is the right grilling method, seasoning and ability to cook to temperature. Using a good quality digital meat thermometer will also take the guesswork out of knowing when your beef shorties are ready. Another important step is spritzing the ribs during the cook, so make sure you have a spray bottle on hand. Our beef rub is packed full of flavor without being overpowering, so you still get to taste the hearty, beefy goodness of these tender, juicy ribs.

BEEF RUB
2 tbsp (12 g) mustard powder

1 tbsp (8 g) garlic powder

2 tsp (5 g) onion powder

2 tsp (3 g) cayenne pepper

1 tbsp (18 g) kosher salt

2 tsp (4 g) ground black pepper

2 tbsp (14 g) ground sweet paprika

2 tbsp (28 g) soft brown sugar

1 tbsp (7 g) cracked pepper

RIBS
2 (3-bone) beef short ribs (ask your butcher for trimmed plate short ribs)

2 tbsp (30 ml) olive oil

SPRITZING MIXTURE
¾ cup (180 ml) apple cider vinegar

¾ cup (180 ml) apple juice

To make the Beef Rub, mix the mustard powder, garlic powder, onion powder, cayenne pepper, kosher salt, ground pepper, sweet paprika, brown sugar and cracked pepper until well combined.

Trim any excess fat; if you leave too much on the ribs, the fat won't render down. Remove the thin membrane from the bone side of the ribs, using a butter knife to loosen the membrane above the bone and a paper towel to remove it completely, away from the bone. The paper towel will help you grip the membrane more easily. This is an important step because the membrane gets very tough when cooked and won't break down as the ribs cook. Not only will the seasoning not penetrate properly through the membrane, but there's nothing worse than trying to bite through it when diving in to enjoy the beef ribs.

Coat the ribs with the olive oil and season them with the beef rub. Then allow the ribs to reach room temperature. Meanwhile, make the Spritzing Mixture by adding the apple cider vinegar and apple juice to a spray bottle. Set it aside until needed.

(continued)

BEEF SHORT RIBS *with*
BOURBON BBQ SAUCE *(continued)*

BOURBON BBQ SAUCE

1½ cups (360 ml) ketchup

1 cup (220 g) brown sugar

⅓ cup (80 ml) good quality bourbon whisky

¼ cup (60 ml) cold water

2 tbsp (30 ml) Worcestershire sauce

2 tbsp (30 ml) apple cider vinegar

2 tbsp (30 ml) pure maple syrup

2 tbsp (28 g) cold butter, chopped

1 tsp onion powder

1 tsp garlic powder

2 tsp (4 g) mustard powder

1 tsp salt

½ tsp pepper

½ tsp cayenne pepper

For the bourbon sauce, to a small saucepan on the stove, add the ketchup, brown sugar, whisky, water, Worcestershire sauce, apple cider vinegar, maple syrup, butter, onion powder, garlic powder, mustard powder, salt, pepper and cayenne pepper. Combine well and then simmer gently for 15 minutes, stirring occasionally.

Prepare a Traeger grill by turning it to the SMOKE setting. Wait about 5 minutes for it to produce smoke, then set the Traeger to run at 250°F (120°C).

Cook the ribs for at least 7 hours. After the first hour, spritz the ribs every 30 minutes until the ribs are ready to be wrapped in your choice of butcher paper or aluminium foil (see next paragraph). This will prevent them from drying out.

When the ribs reach an internal temperature of 170°F (75°C), they might begin to stall. This means the internal temperature will remain the same and not rise for a while. It's then time to do the Texas Crutch method. To do this, remove the ribs from the grill and wrap them tightly with butcher paper. Wrapping the ribs will get the temperature rising again by trapping the moisture and keeping the beef juicy. We like to use food-grade butcher paper because we're able to achieve a nice bark on the ribs. When we use aluminium foil, the bark softens because the moisture isn't able to escape the way it can when using butcher paper.

The ribs are ready when the internal temperature reaches 205°F (95°C). It's important to note that the connective tissue will not begin to break down until you're 5 to 6 hours into the cook. Be patient and remember, time is your best friend when it comes to perfect beef ribs.

Rest the ribs for 30 minutes before slicing. Serve them with the homemade Bourbon BBQ Sauce.

 NOTE: For saucy ribs, brush them with the Bourbon BBQ Sauce 30 minutes before removing them from the grill.

TENDER LAMB RIBS *with* PURPLE SLAW

YIELD
4 servings

Your taste buds will be thanking you when you bite into these tender lamb ribs, enjoyed with a side of our creamy purple slaw. Like a lot of our recipes, the marinade and purple slaw can be prepared ahead of time. You only need to sit back and enjoy the aromas in your backyard as you cook the lamb low and slow for 3 hours. It's worth the wait for these tender, mouth-watering ribs. Cook these on the grill of your choice—as long as you can cook them low and slow . . . you're good to go! Get ready for some tasty lamb ribs that are crispy on the outside and super tender on the inside.

LAMB MARINADE

⅓ cup (80 ml) olive oil

2 tbsp (32 g) concentrated tomato paste

2 tbsp (30 ml) lemon juice

2 cloves garlic, crushed

2 tsp (5 g) ground sweet paprika

1 tbsp (3 g) dried rosemary

¼ tsp cumin

1 tsp onion powder

1 tsp salt

1 tsp pepper

1.7 lb (800 g) lamb ribs

PURPLE SLAW

½ cup (120 ml) mayonnaise

½ cup (120 ml) sour cream

1 tbsp (15 ml) apple cider vinegar

2 tbsp (30 ml) lemon juice

2 tsp (10 ml) honey

1 tsp Dijon mustard

½ tsp salt

½ tsp white pepper

1 small purple cabbage, thinly shredded

SPRITZING MIXTURE

½ cup (120 ml) apple cider

½ cup (120 ml) water

To make the marinade, in a large bowl, mix the olive oil, tomato paste, lemon juice, garlic, paprika, rosemary, cumin, onion powder, salt and pepper.

Trim the lamb ribs of the fat cap on one side. The fat cap is a flap of fat that covers half the ribs. Leave about ¼ inch (6 mm) of fat on the remainder of the ribs to help keep them moist and add flavor. We recommend removing the thin membrane from the bone side of the ribs, using a butter knife to loosen the membrane above the bone and a paper towel to remove it completely, pulling it away from the bone. The paper towel helps grip the membrane more easily. This is an important step because the membrane gets very tough when cooked and won't break down. Pat the ribs dry and add them to a baking tray, then coat them with the marinade. Refrigerate, covered, for at least 4 hours or overnight.

For the slaw, whisk the mayonnaise, sour cream, apple cider vinegar, lemon juice, honey, mustard, salt and white pepper. Place the shredded purple cabbage in a large bowl and add the dressing, then toss to combine. Refrigerate the slaw until needed.

Make the Spritzing Mixture by adding the apple cider vinegar and water to a spray bottle. Set it aside until needed.

(continued)

Prepare a grill for indirect heat (see the Frequently Asked Grilling Questions section on page 10) and preheat it to 225°F (105°C). To add a smoky flavor, you can add some wood chunks to charcoal, use a smoke box filled with wood chips in a gas grill or choose your favorite wood pellets for a pellet grill.

Place the ribs, bone-side down, directly on the grill grate or on a baking rack that's suitable for a barbecue. Cook the ribs for 3 hours or until the internal temperature reaches a minimum of 145°F (65°C), spraying them with the spritzing mixture every 30 minutes. They don't need to be wrapped during the cook. The meat will shrink back from the ends when they're ready.

Rest the ribs for 10 minutes and serve with the Purple Slaw.

ZESTY MINTED LAMB CUTLETS *with* CREAMY GARLIC MASH

YIELD
4 servings

Our tender, juicy lamb cutlets served over a creamy, garlic mash is such a versatile recipe. It's just as ideal for those busy weeknights when you need a satisfying meal, fast, as it is on a weekend when an impressive dish needs to be served to your guests. We've added a delicious onion gravy that complements the lamb and takes the garlic mash to another level.

ZESTY MINTED LAMB MARINADE

⅓ cup (30 g) fresh mint, finely chopped

1 tbsp (2 g) fresh lemon thyme leaves

2 cloves garlic, crushed

½ tsp sweet paprika

¼ cup (60 ml) fresh lemon juice

¼ cup (60 ml) olive oil

1 tsp sea salt

½ tsp cracked pepper

8 lamb cutlets

CREAMY GARLIC MASH

8 starchy potatoes, cut into 1-inch (2.5-cm) cubes

1½ tsp (9 g) sea salt, divided

3 cloves garlic, crushed

½ cup (120 ml) heavy whipping cream

¼ cup (57 g) butter

¼ tsp ground nutmeg

1 tsp finely chopped chives

ONION GRAVY

1 tsp olive oil

1 yellow onion, sliced

1 cup (240 ml) chicken stock

1 tbsp (14 g) butter

1 tsp cornstarch

3 tbsp (45 ml) water

To make the zesty minted marinade, to a large ziptop bag add the mint, thyme, garlic, sweet paprika, lemon juice, olive oil, salt and pepper. Add the lamb cutlets to the ziptop bag, seal the bag and make sure the cutlets are well coated with the marinade. Refrigerate for 4 hours or overnight.

Prepare a gas grill or kettle for direct grilling, and preheat it to 375°F (190°C), with the lid down. To cook the lamb cutlets, heat a skillet on the grill. It should be hot enough that there should be a sizzle as soon as you place the lamb cutlets on the skillet. This will create a nice sear. Cook the lamb cutlets for approximately 4 minutes per side, until the internal temperature reaches 145°F (65°C). Remove the lamb from the grill, cover it with foil and allow the meat to rest for 5 minutes before you serve it. Set aside the skillet for cooking the gravy later, reserving any pan juices.

While the lamb is cooking, make the Creamy Garlic Mash. Add the potatoes to a large pot, cover them with cold water, and add 1 teaspoon of the salt. Place the pot on the grill and bring the water to a boil, then reduce the heat and simmer the potatoes for 15 minutes or until they're tender. Check for doneness by sliding a skewer into the center of a potato. If it slides out easily without resistance, they are ready. Drain the water and mash the potatoes with a potato ricer or fork. Using a potato ricer will produce a fluffy and smooth mash. Mix in the garlic, remaining ½ teaspoon salt, cream, butter, nutmeg and chives, cover with foil and set aside while you make the gravy.

Use the same skillet the lamb cutlets were cooked in to make the Onion Gravy. The leftover juices from the lamb cutlets will give it even more flavor. With the skillet over medium heat, add the olive oil and sauté the onions for about 5 minutes or until they become translucent. Then pour in the chicken stock and add the butter. Simmer for 10 minutes, stirring occasionally. Mix the cornstarch with water in a small cup until there are no lumps. Slowly add the cornstarch liquid to the pan, while stirring. When the sauce starts to thicken, in approximately 7 minutes, remove the pan from the heat. Serve the lamb cutlets on top of the mash, with the Onion Gravy.

MOROCCAN LAMB RACK *with* RED WINE POMEGRANATE SAUCE

YIELD
4 servings

The aromatic spices used to create the Moroccan marinade for the lamb rack and the little bursts of deliciousness from the pomegranate red wine sauce are a perfect match. We always make extra Red Wine Pomegranate Sauce and use it on other barbecued meats as well. It can be stored in the refrigerator for a couple of days and heated up as needed.

MOROCCAN MARINADE

3 tbsp (45 ml) olive oil

2 tbsp (30 ml) fresh lemon juice

1 tbsp (15 ml) honey

2 cloves garlic, crushed

½ tsp ground cumin

1 tsp ground coriander

½ tsp ground turmeric

½ tsp ground cinnamon

¼ tsp cayenne pepper

1 tsp sweet paprika

1 tsp sea salt

2 lamb racks, French trimmed, 4 ribs each

RED WINE POMEGRANATE SAUCE (MAKES 1 CUP [240 ML])

1 tbsp (15 ml) olive oil

1 medium onion, finely diced

2 cups (480 ml) full-bodied red wine such as Merlot

½ cup (120 ml) pomegranate juice

½ cup (120 ml) chicken stock

1 tsp cornstarch

2 tsp (10 ml) water

3 sprigs fresh lemon thyme

2 tsp (8 g) brown sugar

¼ cup (57 g) butter

2 tbsp (22 g) pomegranate seeds (optional)

In a large ziptop bag, combine the olive oil, lemon juice, honey, garlic, cumin, coriander, turmeric, cinnamon, cayenne pepper, sweet paprika and salt. Add the lamb racks to the ziptop bag, seal the bag and coat the lamb racks all over with the marinade. Refrigerate for 4 hours or overnight.

Prepare a gas grill or kettle for direct grilling and preheat it to 375°F (190°C) for 10 minutes with the lid down.

Start the Red Wine Pomegranate Sauce on the grill. To a medium cast-iron skillet on the grill, add the olive oil and onion. Sauté on medium heat for 2 minutes or until the onion is translucent. Turn up the heat to high, and boil the wine, pomegranate juice and chicken stock until it reduces by half. This will take around 13 minutes. Lower the heat to low. In a small cup, stir the cornstarch and the water until no lumps remain, then pour the mixture into the skillet along with the thyme sprigs. Stir until the sauce begins to thicken; this should only take 1 to 2 minutes. Take the skillet off the heat. Stir in the brown sugar and butter until combined. Put a lid on the skillet to keep the sauce warm and set aside.

Turn the grill up to medium-high. To keep the rib bones from burning, cover them each with a small piece of foil during the cook. Place the lamb racks on the grill grate, meat-side down, and cook for 4 minutes, then flip the racks over and cook for an additional 4 minutes. Move the lamb racks to indirect heat for an additional 15 minutes. The lamb racks are ready to take off the grill when the internal temperature reaches 145°F (65°C). Cover the lamb with foil and allow the meat to rest for 5 minutes before you carve it. Serve with the Red Wine Pomegranate Sauce and pomegranate seeds.

REVERSE SEARED RIBEYE *with* ROASTED GARLIC & ROSEMARY BUTTER

YIELD
2 servings

The secret to cooking a restaurant quality, thick, ribeye steak is to use a grill and the reverse sear method. This recipe will satisfy your inner carnivore and you'll learn how to achieve the perfect steak that's evenly cooked and pink from edge to edge. You might not end up using all the butter, but this is an amazing butter to keep in the freezer and use when needed. You can also substitute the ribeye in this recipe for a big tomahawk, as it works just as well. Follow our recipe and this method for steaks and you won't need to go to a fancy restaurant to enjoy an amazing steak.

RIBEYE

2 (1-lb [454-g]) ribeye steaks

1 tbsp (15 ml) olive oil

2 tsp (12 g) kosher salt

2 tsp pepper

ROASTED GARLIC AND ROSEMARY BUTTER

1 bulb garlic

1 tsp olive oil

7 tbsp (100 g) butter, softened

¼ cup (7 g) fresh rosemary leaves, finely chopped

Coat the steaks with the olive oil and season them with salt and pepper. Allow the steaks to reach room temperature (this will take about 45 minutes).

To roast the garlic, preheat the grill and set to medium-high. Place the garlic bulb on a square piece of aluminium foil and pull up the sides of the foil and scrunch to seal it into a parcel. Roast the garlic on the grill for 20 to 30 minutes or until it feels soft. Remove the parcel from the grill and allow it to cool. Then slice the top off the roasted garlic bulb and set aside.

To prepare the Roasted Garlic and Rosemary Butter, over a small bowl, squeeze the garlic from the bulb. Add the olive oil, butter and rosemary to the bowl and mix until well combined. Transfer the butter mixture to a sheet of cling wrap and shape into a log, twisting the ends of the plastic to seal. Place the butter in the freezer for at least 30 minutes before using.

To reverse sear the steaks, prepare a grill for indirect heat (see the Frequently Asked Grilling Questions section on page 10) and preheat it to 350°F (175°C). Place the steaks on the grill grate on the indirect side, opposite the heat. Close the lid and cook the steaks for 30 minutes, flipping them after 15 minutes. To achieve a medium-rare doneness, once the steak reaches an internal temperature of 125°F (50°C), move the steaks over direct heat and sear them with the grill lid open for 1 to 2 minutes a side, forming a delicious crust. Remove the steaks from the grill when the internal temperature reaches 135°F (60°C). Let the steaks rest for 10 to 15 minutes topped with the Roasted Garlic and Rosemary Butter. Serve the steaks whole or sliced.

Perfect
PORK & CHICKEN

When we grill pork and chicken, our aim is to achieve succulent and tasty meals everyone will love. They are popular meats to barbecue as they can be transformed in so many ways.

In this chapter we will be using a few different techniques, such as searing, grilling low and slow, frying, the indirect method and even cooking pasta using a grill. All these methods will achieve exceptional flavors.

We've included our secret to finger licking fried chicken (page 63), the stickiest pork ribs (page 57), a South American inspired BBQ roast chicken (page 58), an amazing chicken satay (page 68), our favorite easy glazed ham recipe (page 75) and more!

SEARED CHICKEN SKEWERS *with* HARISSA SAUCE

YIELD
4 servings,
12 skewers

Time to turn up the heat with our seared chicken and (very spicy) Harissa Sauce. This recipe is quite versatile. You have the mild aromatic spices coming through from the chicken tenders and then the big bold chili hit from the Harissa Sauce. We always like to serve the Harissa Sauce on the side, as a little goes a long way with this pungent chili sauce—and as a bonus, you can make the sauce up to two weeks ahead of time and keep it in the fridge. If you are using wooden skewers as we have, always remember to soak them in water for 30 minutes prior to grilling so they don't burn.

HARISSA SAUCE

1 oz (28 g) dried whole red chilies

2 cloves garlic

2 tsp (12 g) sea salt

2 tsp (4 g) ground coriander

2 tsp (4 g) ground cumin

¼ cup (60 ml) olive oil

1 tsp fresh parsley, chopped

2 tbsp (30 ml) fresh lemon juice

1 tbsp (15 ml) water

CHICKEN

1 tbsp (8 g) garlic powder

1 tbsp (7 g) sweet paprika

1 tbsp (7 g) cumin

1 tsp ground coriander

1½ tsp (9 g) sea salt

½ tsp pepper

3 tbsp (45 ml) olive oil

2 lb (907 g) chicken tenders

FOR SERVING

2 tbsp (2 g) fresh cilantro leaves

1 lime, cut into wedges

To make the Harissa Sauce, remove the stems from the chilies, then cut them in half lengthways and discard the seeds. Cover the chilies with boiling water from a kettle (or boil it in a small pot) and let them sit for 5 minutes to soften.

Drain the chilies and add them to a small food processor with the garlic, salt, coriander, cumin, olive oil, parsley, lemon juice and water. Blend until well combined. Put the sauce in an airtight container and refrigerate until you're ready to use it. It will keep in the refrigerator for up to 2 weeks, but make sure to bring it to room temperature before using it.

To make the marinade, in a medium bowl, whisk the garlic powder, sweet paprika, cumin, coriander, salt, pepper and olive oil. Pat the tenders dry with a paper towel. Add the marinade and the chicken tenders to a large ziptop bag and seal. Massage the chicken so the marinade has evenly coated all the tenders. Refrigerate for 30 minutes or overnight.

Take the chicken tenders out of the refrigerator and thread each one onto a skewer ready for the grill.

Prepare a gas or charcoal grill for direct heat and preheat it to 375°F (190°C) with the lid down.

Place the chicken skewers on the grill, turning occasionally. Cook for 3 to 4 minutes per side, until the internal temperature of the chicken is 165°F (75°C) and the juices run clear.

Serve with the fresh cilantro and lime wedges and the Harissa Sauce on the side.

Family Favorite
STICKIEST PORK RIBS

YIELD
4 to 6
servings

These pork ribs are sticky, tender and very tasty. This is a recipe you'll make over and over because your friends and family will love it! Just allow 2 hours because we can't stress enough that grilling low and slow requires your time and patience. Let us assure you, though, it's worth the wait for the stickiest and most delicious ribs you'll ever eat.

RIBS

3 lb (1.4 kg) pork ribs (spareribs or baby back ribs)

2 tbsp (30 ml) olive oil

PORK RIB SEASONING

1 tbsp (7 g) ground sweet paprika (or smoked paprika)

2 tsp (5 g) onion powder

2 tsp (5 g) garlic powder

1 tsp ground cumin

1 tsp celery salt

1 tsp kosher salt

1 tsp pepper

STICKY SAUCE

1½ cups (360 ml) ketchup

½ cup (120 ml) apple cider vinegar

¼ cup (60 ml) honey

2 tbsp (30 ml) Worcestershire sauce

1 tbsp (15 ml) pure maple syrup

2 tbsp (28 g) brown sugar

1 tsp onion powder

1 tsp garlic powder

1 tsp salt

1 tsp pepper

SPRITZING MIXTURE

¾ cup (180 ml) apple cider vinegar

¾ cup (180 ml) apple juice

Clean and pat the pork rib racks dry with a paper towel. Remove the thin membrane from the bone side of the ribs. Using a butter knife, loosen the membrane above the bone and use a paper towel to remove it completely, pulling it away from the bone. The paper towel helps grip the membrane more easily. If the membrane is left on the ribs, it won't break down during the cooking process and isn't easy to chew.

To make the rub, in a small bowl, mix the paprika, onion powder, garlic powder, cumin, celery salt, kosher salt and pepper. Apply the olive oil over both sides of the ribs then coat them with the rub and place them in a pan. Leave them, covered, overnight in the refrigerator or for a minimum of 4 hours. The longer you leave them, the more flavor the ribs will take on.

To make the Sticky Sauce, use a gas side burner, set to low heat. In a medium saucepan, stir the ketchup, apple cider vinegar, honey, Worcestershire sauce, maple syrup, brown sugar, onion powder, garlic powder, salt and pepper. Bring to a gentle simmer for 10 minutes, stirring frequently. Remove once the sauce has thickened slightly.

Meanwhile, make the Spritzing Mixture by adding the apple cider vinegar and apple juice to a spray bottle. Set it aside until needed.

Prepare a grill for indirect heat (see the Frequently Asked Grilling Questions section on page 10) and preheat it to approximately 230°F (110°C). Cook the ribs low and slow for 2 hours. During the cook, spray with the Spritzing Mixture every 20 minutes to keep the ribs from drying out. Brush the ribs with the Sticky Sauce during the final 30 minutes and wrap the rib racks individually and tightly with butcher paper or aluminium foil. Continue to cook the ribs until the internal temperature reaches 204°F (95°C).

Let the ribs rest for 15 minutes and serve with more Sticky Sauce on the side.

Citrus CHIMICHURRI ROAST CHICKEN

YIELD
4 servings

We're bringing zesty South American flavors to this succulent roast chicken by serving it with a fresh citrus chimichurri sauce that's bursting with flavor and also acts as a condiment. When you add the element of barbecue to chicken, it ends up crispy-skinned, juicy and with a perfect char-grilled taste. Our citrus chimichurri roast chicken is just as delicious served hot out of the grill or cold in a salad. It's one of our favorite roast chicken recipes and we think you'll love it too.

CITRUS CHIMICHURRI SAUCE

1½ cups (90 g) fresh parsley leaves, chopped

1 cup (16 g) fresh cilantro, chopped

2 tbsp (7 g) fresh oregano, chopped

3 cloves garlic, crushed

1 lemon, juiced

1 orange, juiced

1 cup (240 ml) olive oil

¼ cup (60 ml) red wine vinegar

1 tsp salt

¼ tsp pepper

CHICKEN SEASONING

1 tbsp (7 g) sweet paprika

1 tbsp (6 g) ground cumin

2 tsp (5 g) garlic powder

1 tsp dried oregano

1 tsp salt

½ tsp pepper

CHICKEN

1 (4½-lb [1.8-kg]) whole chicken

2 tbsp (30 ml) olive oil

Potatoes, pumpkin or carrots, for roasting (optional)

To make the Citrus Chimichurri Sauce, add the parsley, cilantro, oregano, garlic, lemon juice, orange juice, olive oil, red wine vinegar, salt and pepper to a food processor. Pulse until all the ingredients are chopped, well combined and smooth. If you prefer a chunky sauce, pulse for less time. This sauce can also be made ahead of time, if needed, and kept in the refrigerator for 3 days. Divide the sauce into two equal portions—one will be to baste the chicken as soon as it comes out of the grill and one will be to serve.

To make the Chicken Seasoning, in a small bowl, mix the sweet paprika, cumin, garlic powder, oregano, salt and pepper.

Wipe and pat dry the chicken with a paper towel. Place the chicken in a baking tray and coat the chicken (including the cavity) with the olive oil and then the Chicken Seasoning. Feel free to add potatoes, pumpkin or carrots to the baking tray if you'd like. Cover the chicken with cling wrap and refrigerate for at least 3 hours or overnight.

Prepare a grill for indirect heat (see the Frequently Asked Grilling Questions section on page 10) and preheat it to 390°F (200°C). Cook the chicken for 1 to 1½ hours with the grill lid closed, until the juices run clear and an internal temperature of 165°F (75°C) is reached. For an accurate reading, place the meat thermometer in the thickest part of the chicken.

When the chicken is cooked, remove it from the grill, brush it all over with the first portion of Citrus Chimichurri Sauce and let it rest for 10 to 15 minutes. The resting of the cooked chicken allows for the juices to redistribute, which results in juicer flesh. Serve the whole roast chicken with a side of the second portion of Citrus Chimichurri Sauce.

WORLD'S BEST BBQ CHICKEN WINGS *with* RANCH DIPPING SAUCE

YIELD
22 to
26 wings

We've never met a person who doesn't love our BBQ chicken wings. We use our special chicken wing rub to season them and then give them a tender loving brush of our homemade BBQ sauce. They're succulent and full of flavor on the inside and sticky and sweet on the outside. The ranch dressing is zesty and creamy—the perfect dipping sauce to have on hand for these yummy wings.

CHICKEN WINGS

2 tsp (5 g) garlic powder

2 tsp (5 g) onion powder

2 tbsp (14 g) smoked paprika

2 tsp (4 g) ground cumin

2 tsp (8 g) soft brown sugar

2 tsp (12 g) salt

1 tsp pepper

2 lb (907 kg) chicken wings, separated into drumettes and flats

2 tbsp (30 ml) olive oil

RANCH DRESSING

½ cup (120 ml) mayonnaise

½ cup (120 ml) sour cream

¼ cup (60 ml) buttermilk, plus more if needed

1 tsp onion powder

2 tsp (2 g) fresh dill, chopped

1 clove garlic, crushed

1 tbsp (15 ml) fresh lemon juice

1 tbsp (3 g) chives, chopped

½ tsp fresh parsley, chopped

¼ tsp sea salt

¼ tsp cracked pepper

Prepare a gas grill for indirect heat (see the Frequently Asked Grilling Questions section on page 10) and preheat it to 350°F (175°C).

To make the rub for the wings, in a large bowl, mix the garlic powder, onion powder, smoked paprika, cumin, brown sugar, salt and pepper. Coat the chicken wings with the olive oil then add them to the bowl with the rub mixture. Ensure the wings are coated evenly with the rub and then refrigerate them for at least 20 minutes.

Meanwhile, to make the Ranch Dressing, in a small bowl, whisk the mayonnaise, sour cream, buttermilk, onion powder, dill, garlic, lemon juice, chives, parsley, salt and pepper until well combined. Refrigerate until needed. This ranch dressing can be made one week ahead and will thicken slightly. Add a tablespoon (15 ml) of buttermilk before using if you don't want it as thick.

(continued)

BBQ SAUCE

2 tbsp (30 ml) olive oil

1 small onion, finely diced

1 tbsp (15 ml) malt vinegar

1 tbsp (15 ml) apple cider vinegar

1 tbsp (14 g) soft brown sugar

1 tbsp (15 ml) honey

⅓ cup (80 ml) ketchup

1 tbsp (15 ml) Worcestershire sauce

To make the BBQ Sauce, use the barbecue side burner and a medium saucepan. Add the olive oil and the onion to the saucepan, then sauté until soft over medium heat for about 5 minutes. Add the malt vinegar, apple cider vinegar, brown sugar, honey, ketchup and Worcestershire sauce. Simmer gently over low heat for 5 minutes, stirring occasionally. Remove the sauce from the heat and allow it to cool slightly. Add the sauce to a blender and pulse until smooth. Set aside until needed.

Place the chicken wings on the grill and cook for 30 to 45 minutes, turning frequently, until they are golden in color and crispy. Then, brush the wings with the BBQ Sauce and continue to cook the wings for about 15 minutes.

Serve the chicken wings warm with a side of Ranch Dressing.

 NOTE: If you want the chicken wings to have a smoky flavor, you can add a smoke box filled with presoaked wood chips throughout the cook if using a gas grill. If you are using a charcoal grill, add wood chunks to the charcoal.

FINGER LICKING FRIED CHICKEN WINGS *with* CREAMY MUSTARD SAUCE

YIELD
3–4
servings

This is one of those recipes that has everyone coming back for seconds and thirds. The combination of herbs, spices and crunch in every bite makes this recipe super special. We find that having a mixture of all-purpose flour and panko breadcrumbs gives an extra crunch to the chicken, and the buttermilk helps break down the protein in the meat and tenderizes the chicken.

We also like making extra rub and storing it in an airtight container so we can use it at any time; it's also great on any other meat or seafood, too. In this recipe we've used the wing of the chicken, but you can use any part you choose.

CHICKEN

2 lb (907 g) chicken wings, separated into drumettes and flats

2 cups (480 ml) buttermilk

CREAMY MUSTARD SAUCE

1 cup (240 ml) chicken stock

1 tbsp (15 ml) white wine vinegar

1 tbsp (15 ml) wholegrain mustard

1 tbsp (15 ml) Dijon mustard

1 tsp dried tarragon leaves

1 cup (240 ml) sour cream

1 tbsp (8 g) cornstarch

3 tbsp (45 ml) water

2 green onions, finely chopped

Kosher salt, to taste

Cracked black pepper, to taste

Clean the chicken wings and pat them dry with a paper towel.

Place the wings in a bowl and cover them with the buttermilk. Cover the bowl and refrigerate for at least 30 minutes, or overnight.

Make the Creamy Mustard Sauce on a barbecue side burner. Add the stock, vinegar, wholegrain mustard, Dijon mustard and tarragon to a small saucepan, over medium heat. Boil until the liquid has reduced by half. This will take approximately 5 minutes. Add the sour cream and stir to combine, making sure the mixture doesn't come to a boil. Mix the cornstarch with the water in a small bowl, then slowly add the mixture to the saucepan while stirring, so no lumps form. The sauce should start to thicken. Remove from the heat and add the green onions, salt and pepper. Transfer the sauce to a bowl and refrigerate until needed.

(continued)

RUB

1 cup (125 g) all-purpose flour
1 cup (70 g) panko breadcrumbs
2 tsp (12 g) sea salt
1 tbsp (3 g) dried thyme
1½ tbsp (8 g) ground sage
1 tsp dried basil
1 tsp dried oregano
1½ tbsp (10 g) sweet paprika
1 tbsp (16 g) garlic salt
2 tsp (5 g) onion powder
1 tsp ground turmeric
1 tbsp (7 g) dried mustard powder
1 tbsp (14 g) celery salt
1 tbsp (5 g) ground ginger
1 tsp black cracked pepper
1 tbsp (7 g) ground white pepper
1 egg
4 cups (960 ml) vegetable oil

To make the rub mixture, to a large plastic ziptop bag, add the flour, breadcrumbs, salt, thyme, sage, basil, oregano, sweet paprika, garlic salt, onion powder, turmeric, mustard powder, celery salt, ginger, black pepper and white pepper. Seal up the bag then shake until the ingredients are well combined. Set aside until needed.

Whisk the egg in a small bowl, then stir it into the bowl containing the chicken wings and buttermilk. Remove one wing at a time from the buttermilk–egg mixture and shake off the excess liquid. Place the wing into the bag with the rub mixture and coat it all over, then set it aside on a plate. Continue until all the wings have been coated.

Prepare a gas grill or kettle for indirect heat (see the Frequently Asked Grilling Questions section on page 10) and preheat it to 375°F (190°C).

Place a wok or deep pot on the grill. Add the vegetable oil. If using a thermometer, heat the vegetable oil until it reaches 180°F (80°C). You can also test the oil by adding a small pinch of the rub to the oil. If it sizzles, it is the right temperature for frying.

Gently drop the chicken wings into the hot oil in batches, and deep fry until golden brown (approximately 3 to 4 minutes). The internal temperature should be 165°F (75°C) and juices should be clear if you cut into the chicken. Place the chicken wings on a paper towel to absorb any excess oil and serve with the Creamy Mustard Sauce.

 NOTES: We triple the dry ingredients and store it in a jar for fast future use on any meats. The Creamy Mustard Sauce can be made a few days ahead and stored in an airtight container in the refrigerator.

SUCCULENT PORK CHOPS *with* APPLE & FENNEL SLAW

YIELD
4 servings

This crispy salad with aniseed-flavored fennel combined with apples gives the pork chop dish that extra punch. The hint of honey and lemon in the dressing makes this salad refreshing, as well as hearty and ideal for summer barbecue gatherings.

PORK CHOPS
1 tsp brown sugar

1 tsp smoked paprika

1 tsp onion powder

1 tsp garlic powder

1 tsp dried thyme

1 tsp ground cumin

1 tsp sea salt

½ tsp black pepper

4 pork chops, bone in or boneless (at least 1 inch [2.5 cm] thick)

¼ cup (60 ml) olive oil

APPLE AND FENNEL SLAW
1 large fennel bulb, thinly sliced

2 cups (140 g) cabbage, thinly sliced

1 red onion, thinly sliced

2 tbsp (7 g) fresh dill, chopped

2 tbsp (8 g) fresh parsley, chopped

2 large apples, cored, quartered and thinly sliced

½ tsp lemon juice

DRESSING
2 tbsp (30 ml) fresh lemon juice

1 tbsp (15 ml) apple cider vinegar

¼ cup (60 ml) olive oil

1 tbsp (15 ml) honey

½ tsp Dijon mustard

½ tsp sea salt

To make the rub for the pork chops, in a small bowl mix the brown sugar, smoked paprika, onion powder, garlic powder, thyme, cumin, salt and pepper. Coat the pork chops with the olive oil and apply the rub all over each chop. Place them all on a plate and cover with cling wrap. Refrigerate for at least 30 minutes or preferably overnight.

To make the Apple and Fennel Slaw, in a large bowl combine the fennel, cabbage, onion, dill and parsley. Before adding the sliced apples to the salad, coat them with the lemon juice to prevent them from turning brown, then add them to the bowl. Set the complete salad aside in the fridge until just ready to serve. The salad can be made a few hours ahead of time, but only add the dressing when you are ready to serve so the salad will stay nice and crisp.

To make the dressing, in a small bowl, whisk the lemon juice, apple cider vinegar, olive oil, honey, Dijon mustard and salt. The dressing can be made 1 day ahead.

Thirty minutes prior to grilling the pork chops, take them out of the refrigerator to come to room temperature so they can cook evenly.

Preheat a grill for direct heat and preheat it to 390°F (200°C). Cook the seasoned pork chops over direct heat for 8 to 12 minutes. The internal temperature should reach 145°F (65°C). When the desired temperature is reached, allow the pork chops to rest for 3 to 5 minutes.

When ready to serve, add the dressing to the salad and toss to coat. Serve with the pork chops.

CHICKEN SATAY STICKS *with* PEANUT SAUCE

YIELD
12 skewers

We were inspired to create this tasty chicken satay dish after traveling to Southeast Asia a few years ago. In our satay marinade, we use coconut milk. It not only tenderizes the chicken but adds delicious flavor. It's such a perfect marinade to use for grilled chicken. We've used chicken tenderloin but you could also use chicken thighs or breast. The quick and creamy peanut sauce we created to serve with the grilled chicken satay sticks is also great as a dipping sauce for grilled shrimp or grilled vegetables.

CHICKEN SATAY

2 cups (480 ml) coconut milk

1 tbsp (7 g) turmeric

1 tbsp (15 ml) soy sauce

1 tbsp (15 ml) oyster sauce

½ tsp salt

½ tsp pepper

12 chicken tenderloins

12 metal skewers

1 tbsp (15 ml) olive oil

Steamed rice, for serving

PEANUT SAUCE

½ cup (120 ml) coconut milk

½ cup (129 g) smooth peanut butter

½ cup (120 ml) pineapple juice

2 tbsp (30 ml) soy sauce

½ tsp garlic powder

½ tsp onion powder

¼ cup (60 ml) sweet chili sauce

To make the Chicken Satay, place the coconut milk, turmeric, soy sauce, oyster sauce, salt and pepper in a large bowl and whisk until well combined. Add the chicken and mix well to coat it. Cover the bowl with cling wrap and refrigerate for at least 30 minutes or overnight.

For the Peanut Sauce, use the gas side burner of your grill, set to low heat. To a medium saucepan, add the coconut milk, peanut butter, pineapple juice, soy sauce, garlic powder, onion powder and sweet chili sauce. Stir until well combined and simmer gently for 4 to 5 minutes, or until thickened.

Prepare a grill for direct heat with a barbecue hotplate and preheat it to 390°F (200°C). Using a barbecue hotplate will help sear the chicken without flare-ups from the marinade falling directly onto the flames.

Thread one chicken tenderloin on each metal skewer. The metal skewers will help cook the chicken quickly. Drizzle each chicken skewer with the olive oil. Cook the skewers for 6 to 8 minutes, turning frequently, until light gold in color. The internal temperature should reach 167°F (75°C). Serve the Chicken Satay immediately with the Peanut Sauce and steamed rice.

GRILLED CHICKEN BURGER *with* SASSY GUACAMOLE

YIELD
2 servings

The combination of barbecue chicken with the creamy avocado guacamole in this recipe is a match made in heaven. The layers of flavor are absolutely delicious. Biting into this burger with all the juices from the chicken, melted cheese, sassy guacamole and fresh tomato, lettuce and onions makes this burger a winner.

Our secret to the sassiest guacamole is adding Worcestershire sauce. Give this recipe a try and send your taste buds dancing!

CHICKEN BURGER

1 tsp dried thyme

1 tsp onion powder

1 tsp garlic powder

1 tsp sweet paprika

¼ tsp cayenne pepper

½ tsp sea salt

2 tbsp (30 ml) olive oil

1 large chicken breast fillet, sliced in half lengthwise

2 slices Cheddar cheese

2 buns

2 lettuce leaves

2 slices tomato

6 slices red onion

SASSY GUACAMOLE

1 ripe avocado, diced

2 tbsp (30 ml) fresh lime juice

1 clove garlic, crushed

1 small red onion, finely diced

1 tomato, finely diced

3 tbsp (3 g) cilantro, chopped

1 tsp Worcestershire sauce

¼ tsp sea salt

In a small bowl, mix the thyme, onion powder, garlic powder, sweet paprika, cayenne pepper, salt and olive oil, then rub it all over the chicken on both sides. Let the chicken sit in the refrigerator for an hour, or longer if possible.

To make the Sassy Guacamole, add the diced avocado pieces to a bowl. Sprinkle the avocado with the lime juice to help the avocado keep its bright green color. Add the garlic to the avocado pieces and mash with a fork. When the avocado is mashed, add the onion, tomato, cilantro, Worcestershire sauce and salt. Mix well then set aside.

Remove the marinating chicken from the refrigerator. Prepare a grill for direct heat and preheat it to 375°F (190°C) with the lid down. When the grill is hot, place the chicken on the grill and cook for about 10 minutes, turning once. Check carefully to make sure the chicken doesn't burn. Just before the chicken reaches an internal temperature of 165°F (75°C), add a slice of cheese to each piece of chicken, so the cheese melts slightly. The chicken is cooked when the internal temperature is 165°F (75°C) and juices run clear.

Cut the buns in half and toast, cut-side down, on the barbecue for a few minutes. Place the bottom of the bun on a serving plate and add one slice of lettuce, some guacamole, chicken, tomato, onion and a little more guacamole, then add the top of the bun. Secure the burger with a small wooden skewer.

Creamy GRILLED SKILLET CHICKEN SCAMPI PASTA

YIELD
4 servings

There's something special about cooking pasta on the grill, especially this Creamy Grilled Chicken Scampi Pasta. The sweetness from the onion and leek combined with the saltiness of the bacon and white wine infused with the juices of the chicken makes this dish luxuriously rich in flavor. It's a dish that will astonish and delight your guests and it is so easy to prepare outdoors.

1 tbsp (6 g) sea salt

1 lb (454 g) linguine

2 tbsp (30 ml) olive oil

2 large chicken breasts, diced into 1-inch (2.5-cm) pieces

2 tbsp (28 g) butter

1 large onion, diced

1 cup (90 g) leek, diced

2 bacon slices, chopped

5 cloves garlic, crushed

1 cup (149 g) cherry tomatoes, sliced in half

¼ cup (45 g) Kalamata olives, pitted

½ cup (120 ml) dry white wine

1 cup (240 ml) chicken stock

¼ cup (60 ml) heavy whipping cream

1 tbsp (4 g) fresh parsley, chopped for garnish

¼ cup (25 g) grated Parmesan cheese

Prepare a grill for direct heat and preheat it to 375°F (190°C). Place a big pot filled with water and the salt on the grill and let it come to a boil. Add the linguine and cook according to package instructions until al dente. Reserve ½ cup (120 ml) of the pasta water.

Place a large skillet on the grill and add the oil and chicken. Cook the chicken for 7 to 8 minutes over medium heat, stirring occasionally, until it is browned and cooked through. Remove the chicken from the skillet and set it aside.

In the same skillet, melt the butter, then sauté the onion and leeks for 5 minutes, still over medium heat, until they become soft and translucent. Add the chicken pieces, bacon, garlic, cherry tomatoes, olives, wine, chicken stock and the reserved pasta cooking water. Cook for 10 minutes. Add the cream and cook an additional 3 minutes. Serve in a big dish garnished with the parsley and a sprinkle of Parmesan cheese.

EASY GLAZED HAM *for Any Occasion*

YIELD
10 servings

When we're after a spectacular centerpiece everyone can feast on at a special occasion, we prepare our simple glazed ham. The glaze is simple to make but imparts a delicious flavor. We use the grill to cook it, which provides an amazing flavor and frees up indoor oven space—essential when we're feeding a crowd and cooking lots of food. There's also nothing better than glazed ham leftovers eaten hot or cold in sandwiches, just ask our families!

1 (15-lb [7-kg]) leg ham
25 to 30 whole cloves
½ cup (110 g) brown sugar
½ cup (120 ml) maple syrup
½ cup (120 ml) honey
2 tsp (10 ml) Dijon mustard
1 large orange, juiced

Allow the ham 45 minutes to come to room temperature prior to cooking. Place a rack in a roasting tray.

Preheat a grill for indirect heat (see the Frequently Asked Grilling Questions section on page 10) and preheat it to 350°F (180°C). If you're using charcoal, place a drip tray in the center and add 1 cup (240 ml) of water to it. This will prevent flare-ups if the glaze drips directly onto the charcoal.

To prepare the ham, using a sharp knife, cut through the rind at the shank end of the ham and gently lift off the rind by running your fingers between the rind and the fat. Then gently pull off the rind, leaving approximately 4 inches (10 cm) of the skin attached to the shank. Score the fat in diamond patterns all over but don't cut through to the meat. Press a clove into the center of each diamond.

Using the barbecue side burner and a small saucepan, combine the brown sugar, maple syrup, honey, Dijon mustard and orange juice. Simmer the mixture over low heat until it's well combined and the sugar has dissolved.

Place the scored ham onto the rack in the roasting tray. Brush the ham with one-third of the glaze and then wrap the skin on the shank with aluminium foil, to prevent it from burning. Cook for approximately 1 hour to 1½ hours, basting it with the glaze every 30 minutes. You may need to turn the roasting tray halfway through to ensure even cooking.

Remove the ham from the grill and let it rest for 15 minutes. Remove the cloves from the ham prior to slicing. To steady it on the carving board, use a carving fork.

BARBECUED CHICKEN CAPRESE SANDWICH *with* BASIL PESTO

YIELD
4 servings

When you combine grilled chicken, mozzarella, tomatoes and our basil pesto sauce, you get a taste sensation like no other! This is a tasty and satisfying real deal sandwich that we prepare fresh or toasted when we're craving grilled food. For those watching their carb intake, you can skip the bread and still have an amazing meal.

BASIL PESTO

2 cups (48 g) fresh basil leaves

⅓ cup (45 g) pine nuts

2 cloves garlic, crushed

⅓ cup (33 g) finely grated Parmesan cheese

¾ cup (180 ml) olive oil

½ tsp salt

¼ tsp pepper

CAPRESE SANDWICH

2 skinless chicken breasts, halved lengthwise

2 tsp (10 ml) olive oil

1 tsp salt

1 tsp pepper

2 tbsp (30 ml) butter, melted (for basting)

8 slices of ciabatta, toasted

8 slices fresh mozzarella cheese

8 slices fresh tomatoes

In a food processor, pulse the basil leaves, pine nuts, garlic, Parmesan cheese, olive oil, salt and pepper until the basil is chopped finely and well combined.

Coat the chicken with the olive oil and season with the salt and pepper.

Prepare a grill for direct heat and preheat it to 390°F (200°C). Grill the chicken for 6 to 8 minutes a side or until the internal temperate reaches 165°F (75°C). Halfway through, baste the chicken with the melted butter to keep it moist and tasty. When the chicken is cooked, remove it from the grill and allow it to rest for 3 to 5 minutes. Meanwhile, allow the ciabatta slices to toast for 1 to 2 minutes or until you see grill marks.

To build the sandwich, place the grilled chicken on a slice of toasted ciabatta. Layer the sliced mozzarella and tomatoes, then top with a tablespoon (15 g) of basil pesto and another slice of ciabatta.

PORTUGUESE PORK TENDERLOIN *with* PERI PERI SAUCE

YIELD
4 servings

You can have a delicious meal on the dinner table in no time at all by grilling the lean and tasty pork tenderloin cut. For added flavor, we love using our dry rub and accompanying the grilled pork with our tangy and spicy Peri Peri Sauce. Just a little tip: make a double batch of the Peri Peri Sauce, because it's delicious on chicken, too, and keeps well in the fridge for at least 2 weeks. Our Peri Peri Sauce recipe includes a char-grilled onion and bell pepper that we pre-grill for 5 minutes per side on high heat for extra flavor but you don't have to grill them if you're short on time.

PORK TENDERLOIN

2 tbsp (14 g) ground smoked paprika

2 tbsp (8 g) garlic powder

2 tsp (12 g) salt

1 tsp cayenne pepper

1 tbsp (3 g) dried oregano

1 tsp cardamom powder

1 tsp ground allspice

2.5 lbs (1.1 kg) whole pork tenderloins, trimmed (2 pieces)

1 tbsp (15 ml) olive oil

PERI PERI SAUCE

1 red Spanish onion, cut into 2-inch (5-cm) chunks

1 red bell pepper, cut into 2-inch (5-cm) chunks

¼ cup + 2 tbsp (90 ml) olive oil, divided

5 cloves garlic

4 red chilies, African bird's eye or similar

1 tomato, chopped

¼ cup (60 ml) red wine vinegar

2 tsp (2 g) dried oregano

2 tsp (5 g) ground sweet paprika

2 tsp (8 g) brown sugar

2 tsp (12 g) salt

1 tsp pepper

In a small bowl, combine the smoked paprika, garlic powder, salt, cayenne pepper, oregano, cardamom and allspice. Coat the pork with the olive oil and apply the seasoning evenly. Allow the pork to reach room temperature. This will help achieve an evenly cooked tenderloin.

While the pork is reaching room temperature, prepare a grill using a grill grate for direct heat and preheat it to 390°F (200°C). Brush the onion and bell pepper with 2 tablespoons (30 ml) of the olive oil then place them directly on the grill grate. Cook them for 5 to 7 minutes a side. Set them aside until needed.

In a food processor, blend the char-grilled onion, char-grilled bell pepper, garlic, chilies, the remaining ¼ cup (60 ml) of the olive oil, the tomato, red wine vinegar, dried oregano, sweet paprika, brown sugar, salt and pepper. Pulse until the sauce is smooth. Refrigerate until needed.

Cook the pork tenderloin on the grill for approximately 15 to 20 minutes, turning frequently, until an internal temperature of 145°F (65°C) is achieved. Rest the pork, covered loosely with aluminium foil, for 5 minutes. Serve immediately with the Peri Peri Sauce and your preferred sides.

Sensational SEAFOOD

There something about the char-grilled flavor of barbecued seafood that makes it irresistible. It's usually cooked hot and fast for a quick and delicious meal.

Living in Australia, we're blessed to have the best seafood at our doorstep. We've been grilling and cooking amazing seafood for a very long time and know exactly how to grill it perfectly.

We're constantly asked to share our methods and grilling recipes for seafood. Our simple preparation and techniques will transform your seafood dishes into extraordinary meals. Brushing the seafood throughout the cook will keep it nice and moist, and brushing the grill will prevent the seafood from sticking.

In this chapter, we share our best recipes for grilled lobster (page 82), oysters (page 89), Mexican shrimp fajitas (page 91), shrimp po' boys (page 99), flambéed scallops (page 104), seafood paella (page 86) and lots more! Our Luscious Lobster & Bacon Mac 'n' Cheese (page 96) is a family favorite and the Best Garlic Grilled Butterflied Shrimp (page 103) will satisfy any palate. As soon as you're grilling our seafood recipes, the cooking aromas from the grill will tempt the taste buds of any guest!

GRILLED LOBSTER *with* SAFFRON BUTTER

YIELD
2 servings

Lobster and butter are a match made in heaven, but when we add saffron, this exquisite meal is taken to the next level. Lobster is not a difficult crustacean to grill and it's perfect for a romantic dinner at home or when you feel like grilling something extra special. To save time, the entire meal can be prepared ahead of time and kept in the refrigerator until you're ready to cook. We've used fresh lobster in this recipe, but you can buy it frozen and thaw it in the refrigerator overnight.

1 live lobster (1.5–1.8 lb [700–800 g])

2 tsp (10 ml) warm water

30 threads saffron, chopped

⅔ cup (150 g) butter, softened

½ tsp salt

¼ tsp white pepper

2 cloves garlic, minced

1 tsp chopped fresh parsley

2 tsp (10 ml) olive oil

To prepare the lobster, humanely freeze it for a couple of hours before cooking. If you prefer to not buy a live lobster, ask your fishmonger to euthanize it for you or buy a frozen one.

Cut the lobster in half lengthwise by placing it on a chopping board and using a pair of kitchen scissors or a large sharp knife. Remove the stomach sac, which is located behind the mouth, and the intestine, which is in the tail. Refrigerate until needed.

In a small bowl, mix the warm water and saffron threads and leave for 5 minutes so they infuse. Then, in another small bowl, mix the butter, salt, white pepper, garlic, parsley and then add the saffron threads, along with the infused water.

Prepare a grill for direct heat and preheat it to 390°F (200°C). Brush the flesh side of the lobster with the olive oil. Grill the lobster halves, flesh-side down, for 4 to 5 minutes.

Place a cast-iron skillet over high heat or a grill side burner and melt the saffron-infused butter mixture.

Place the grilled lobster halves into the skillet and baste the flesh with the saffron butter for 2 to 3 minutes, or until the flesh is opaque. Don't overcook the lobster or it will become tough. Serve the grilled lobster immediately, topped with the leftover melted saffron butter.

HEAVENLY SEAFOOD PLATTER *with* HOMEMADE COCKTAIL SAUCE

YIELD
4 servings

The secret to serving great seafood is to buy the freshest you can find and not overcook it. We like to serve every kind of grilled seafood with a tasty dressing and a delicious sauce. In this recipe, we have included an amazing dressing that doubles up as a basting mixture and a creamy, tangy sauce that is amazing on all seafood. Serve this seafood platter at your next special occasion and it will surely impress. Or treat yourself to an extra-special grilled seafood night at home.

COCKTAIL SAUCE

½ cup (120 g) mayonnaise

1 tbsp (15 ml) ketchup

2 tsp (10 ml) Worcestershire sauce

3 drops Tabasco sauce

1 tbsp (15 ml) lemon juice

1 tbsp (3 g) fresh dill, finely chopped

SEAFOOD MARINADE AND BASTING MIXTURE

¼ cup (60 ml) olive oil

1 lemon, juiced

2 cloves garlic, crushed

1 tsp dried oregano

1 tsp fresh parsley

Salt and pepper, to taste

SEAFOOD

2 Blue Swimmer crabs, halved and cleaned

4 lobster tails, halved and cleaned

1 lb (454 g) raw shrimp, frozen or fresh

2.2 lb (1 kg) mussels, debearded and rinsed

Lemon wedges, for serving

To make the Cocktail Sauce, in a small bowl, mix the mayonnaise, ketchup, Worcestershire sauce, Tabasco sauce, lemon juice and dill. Combine all the ingredients well and refrigerate until needed. This sauce can be made up to 1 week ahead.

For the Seafood Marinade and Basting Mixture, in a small bowl, whisk the olive oil, lemon juice, garlic, oregano, parsley, salt and pepper. Set aside until needed.

Clean and prepare all the seafood. Pat all the seafood dry with a paper towel.

Prepare a grill for direct heat using a grill grate and preheat it to 390°F (200°C). Have the Seafood Marinade and Basting Mixture on hand for the entire cook and brush all the seafood, except the crabs, frequently. The crabs will stay moist because the flesh is protected from the heat by their shell.

Cook the crabs and lobster tails for 12 to 15 minutes, turning frequently. The lobster tails will need to start cooking shell-side down.

After the first 5 minutes of cooking the crabs and lobster tails, add the shrimp and cook for 3 to 4 minutes a side, until opaque.

Cook the mussels for 2 to 3 minutes, or until they open. When they open, add some basting mixture into the shell and onto the mussel. Discard any shells that do not open.

Remove all the seafood from the grill when ready and arrange on a platter. Serve with the Cocktail Sauce and lemon wedges.

Scrumptious SEAFOOD PAELLA

YIELD
6 servings

Making this scrumptious seafood paella dish, which is famous in Spain, is not as hard as it looks. It is made with a short grain arborio rice, which absorbs all the juices without getting mushy.

This dish gets its name from the large double-handled shallow pan that it is cooked in. If you are not able to find a paella pan, you can also use a large skillet. Paella is a feast for the eyes as well as the stomach, and is a great way to entertain a table full of guests.

2.2 lb (1 kg) live mussels

¼ cup (60 ml) olive oil

1 large onion, diced

½ cup (75 g) diced red bell pepper

½ cup (75 g) diced yellow bell pepper

2 large tomatoes, diced

6 cloves garlic, crushed

5 baby octopus, fresh or frozen, cleaned and beaks removed

4 oz (113 g) squid, cleaned and sliced into rings

5 cups (1.4 L) chicken stock

½ cup (120 ml) dry white wine

2 cups (400 g) arborio rice

1 tsp saffron threads

1.1 lb (500 g) raw shrimp, peeled, deveined, heads and tails left on

12 clams, cleaned

12 scallops (reserve 4 shells for garnish)

¼ tsp sugar (optional)

1 lemon, cut into wedges, for garnish

1 tsp fresh parsley, finely chopped

Under running water, clean the mussels by using a paring knife to scrape off any dirt and pull away the beards. The beards are the strings that hang from the mussel's shell. Discard any broken mussels. If there are any mussels that are open, once you pull away the beard they should close. If any mussels resist being closed, discard them.

Prepare a grill for direct heat and preheat it to 375°F (190°C).

Set a large paella pan or large skillet on the preheated grill. Add the olive oil, onion, red bell pepper and yellow bell pepper and sauté, stirring frequently for 5 minutes. Add the tomatoes and garlic and cook an additional 5 minutes, then add the baby octopus and the squid, stirring gently for 3 minutes.

Pour in the stock and wine, stir well and bring to a boil. Stir in the rice and saffron. Bring the liquid back to a boil, then lower the heat and simmer for 10 minutes.

Gently stir in the shrimp, cleaned mussels, clams and scallops. Taste the liquid to see if you need to add the sugar then cover the pan with a lid, and cook an additional 15 to 20 minutes, until the mussel and clam shells open and the rice is tender. If there are any shells that do not open, discard them. If you don't have a large enough lid, cover the pan with two sheets of foil.

Serve the paella in the pan garnished with lemon wedges, parsley and a few of the scallops in their shells.

BARBECUED OYSTERS *3 Ways*

YIELD
6 servings

The world is truly your oyster with this Barbecued Oysters 3 Ways recipe. Start with the Oysters Kilpatrick; bacon-infused oysters are a great starter. Second, have the Butter, Garlic and Chili Oysters. That little bit of heat kick will have you ready for the cheesy and creamy finish of the Oysters Mornay.

When buying oysters, it's important to always make sure the oysters have been freshly shucked. An easy way to make sure the oysters are fresh is when you smell them, they should smell of the sea.

2 cups (575 g) rock salt or rice to secure oysters on platter

OYSTERS KILPATRICK
12 oysters, shucked

2 rashers bacon

2 tbsp (30 ml) Worcestershire sauce

Fill a tray with the rock salt or rice, and place the shucked, half-shelled oysters on the salt (or rice). This will help steady and secure the oysters so you can add the toppings before grilling.

Prepare a grill for direct medium heat using a grill grate and a hotplate and preheat it to 390°F (200°C).

When grilling, the oysters need to be placed as carefully as possible on the grill grate, so the juices will not fall out and cause flare-ups. The oysters are cooked when the edges of the oyster flesh start to brown slightly—the cooking time will vary by preparation (see below). When the oysters are ready to be taken off the grill, use a pair of long barbecue tongs or heatproof gloves to remove the oysters, as the oyster shells will be very hot.

Use the same platter lined with the rock salt or rice to place the cooked oysters on and serve immediately, as soon as you take them off the grill.

OYSTERS KILPATRICK
On the hotplate, cook the bacon for 3 to 4 minutes or until crispy on each side, then remove. Using scissors, cut the bacon into small cubes and set aside in a bowl.

Add a few drops of Worcestershire sauce and bacon pieces to each of the oysters and place the oysters on the grill grate. The oysters should be ready to come off the grill in 3 to 4 minutes.

(continued)

BUTTER, GARLIC AND CHILI OYSTERS

12 oysters, shucked

1 tbsp (14 g) butter

3 cloves garlic, crushed

2 small chilies, finely chopped (optional)

½ tsp parsley, finely chopped

OYSTERS MORNAY

12 oysters, shucked

¼ cup (60 ml) heavy cream

½ cup (57 g) shredded Cheddar cheese

⅓ cup (27 g) shredded Parmesan cheese

1 tbsp (4 g) fresh parsley, finely chopped

BUTTER, GARLIC AND CHILI OYSTERS

In a small bowl, mix the butter, garlic, chilies (if using) and parsley. Place a small amount of the butter mixture in each of the oysters. Place the oysters onto the grill grate and cook for 3 to 4 minutes.

OYSTERS MORNAY

Add 1 teaspoon of heavy whipping cream, 1 teaspoon of Cheddar cheese and one pinch of Parmesan cheese to each oyster. Place the oysters on the grill grate and cook for 1 to 2 minutes, or until the cheeses are browned and bubbling. Remove them from the grill and sprinkle with the parsley.

MEXICAN SHRIMP FAJITAS *with* HOMEMADE TORTILLAS & LIME CREMA

YIELD
10 servings

We love taking Mexican shrimp fajitas to the next level by making our own soft and tasty tortillas. Nothing compares to homemade tortillas and sizzling shrimp seasoned in our Mexican rub, topped with a creamy lime crema. You won't want to go out for Mexican again! Save time and prepare the Mexican rub, lime crema and tortillas ahead. Then simply grill the seasoned shrimp, bell peppers and onions when you're hungry for magnificent Mexican!

LIME CREMA
1 cup (240 ml) sour cream

⅓ cup (80 ml) mayonnaise

1 clove garlic, crushed

1 lime, juiced and zested

Salt and white pepper, to taste

MEXICAN RUB
2 tbsp (14 g) smoked paprika

1 tbsp (6 g) cumin powder

1 tsp onion powder

1 tsp cayenne pepper

1 tsp ground ginger

1 tsp celery salt

2 tbsp (28 g) brown sugar

1 tbsp (3 g) dried oregano

1 tbsp (18 g) salt

1 tsp white pepper

FAJITAS
25 to 30 large raw shrimp, fresh or frozen, peeled and deveined

1 tbsp (15 ml) olive oil

2 tbsp (30 ml) avocado oil, divided

1 medium red bell pepper, cored and sliced into strips

1 medium green pepper, cored and sliced into strips

1 medium yellow onion, peeled and sliced into thin strips

To make the Lime Crema, in a small bowl, whisk the sour cream, mayonnaise, garlic, lime juice, lime zest, salt and white pepper. Refrigerate until needed.

To make the Mexican Rub, in a small bowl, mix the smoked paprika, cumin, onion powder, cayenne pepper, ginger, celery salt, brown sugar, dried oregano, salt and white pepper. Combine well and set aside until needed.

Place the shrimp in a large bowl, coat them with the olive oil and season generously with the Mexican Rub. Refrigerate the seasoned shrimp for 30 minutes.

(continued)

MEXICAN SHRIMP FAJITAS *with*
HOMEMADE TORTILLAS & LIME CREMA *(continued)*

FLOUR TORTILLAS
2 cups (250 g) all-purpose flour +
⅓ cup (40 g) extra, if needed

1 tsp baking powder

½ tsp salt

¾ cup (180 ml) warm water

2 tbsp (30 ml) melted unsalted butter

FOR SERVING
1 avocado, peeled and sliced

1 cup (113 g) grated Cheddar cheese

⅓ cup (6 g) fresh cilantro, chopped

Fresh lime wedge

To make the Flour Tortillas, to a medium bowl, add the 2 cups (250 g) of flour, baking powder, salt, water and melted butter. Form a dough and knead it on a floured surface for 3 to 5 minutes, until smooth. Use the extra flour if the dough is sticky. Cover the bowl with cling wrap and let the dough rest for 15 minutes. Then divide the dough into ten equal pieces and roll into balls (about the size of Ping-Pong balls). Roll them out into approximately 6-inch (15-cm) diameter circles.

Prepare a grill with a grill grate and hotplate for direct heat and preheat it to 390°F (200°C).

On the hotplate, warm 1 tablespoon (15 ml) of the avocado oil, then cook the bell peppers and onion for 5 minutes, or until soft. Add the remaining 1 tablespoon (15 ml) of avocado oil and the shrimp and cook for another 5 minutes, until the shrimp are opaque. Remove the bell peppers, onions and shrimp from the hotplate and keep warm, covered with aluminium foil.

Using the grill grate, place a skillet over the heat and place a flattened circle tortilla in it. Cook the tortillas, one at a time, for 20 to 40 seconds a side until they bubble slightly. Repeat until all the tortillas are cooked.

Divide the grilled bell peppers, onion and shrimp between the tortillas. Serve with the avocado, cheese, cilantro, a spoonful of lime crema and a lime wedge.

Mouth-Watering MUSSELS IN WHITE WINE & TOMATO SAUCE

YIELD
4 servings

Mussels are not difficult to cook, just a little messy to eat. Always serve this dish with a finger bowl and a bowl for the empty shells. The aromatic sweet flavors of the onion, leek, tomatoes and wine are all you need to create a simple yet delicious meal. Soak up the delicious juices with toasted buttered baguette on the side.

2.2 lb (1 kg) live mussels

3 tbsp (45 g) olive oil

1 onion, diced

½ cup (45 g) leeks, diced

6 cloves garlic, crushed

2 vine tomatoes, diced

½ cup (120 ml) dry white wine

½ tsp sugar

2 tbsp (8 g) fresh parsley, finely chopped

¼ tsp pepper

Salt, to taste

Under running water, clean the mussels by using a paring knife to scrape off any dirt and pull away the beards. The beards are strings that hang from the mussel's shell. Discard any broken mussels. If there are any mussels that are open, once you pull away the beard they should close. If any mussels resist being closed, discard them.

Prepare a gas grill for direct heat and preheat it to 375°F (190°C) with the lid down.

Add the olive oil to a large, deep, cast-iron pan set on the grill. Add the onion and leeks and sauté them for 5 minutes or until they become translucent, then add the tomatoes. Cook an additional 10 minutes, stirring frequently, then add the cleaned mussels, wine, sugar, parsley and pepper. Place the lid on the pan and simmer until all the mussels open. Discard any shells that do not open. Taste the liquid and add the salt to taste, as the mussels can be salty.

Serve immediately.

Luscious LOBSTER & BACON MAC 'N' CHEESE

YIELD
4–6
servings

Everything is better with bacon! Just when we thought our signature mac 'n' cheese couldn't get any tastier, we added lobster and some bacon to add smokiness. This creamy, cheesy and fancy mac 'n' cheese is exquisite. Cooked to golden perfection on the grill, it is sure to impress! This is one of our favorite seafood recipes and can be served as a side or a main.

CRUMB TOPPING
¼ cup (35 g) panko breadcrumbs

¼ cup (25 g) Parmesan cheese

2 tsp (8 g) Simply Delicious Seafood Rub (page 165)

LOBSTER MAC 'N' CHEESE
2 to 3 raw lobster tails, fresh or frozen, cleaned and halved lengthwise

2 tsp (10 ml) olive oil

3 cups (720 ml) heavy whipping cream

2 tbsp (30 ml) crème fraiche

1 clove garlic, crushed

½ tsp salt

¼ tsp pepper

½ cup (57 g) grated sharp Cheddar cheese

1 cup (112 g) grated Havarti cheese (or any easy-melt cheese)

½ cup (57 g) grated Gouda cheese

½ cup (50 g) grated Parmesan cheese

1 tbsp (12 g) Simply Delicious Seafood Rub (page 165)

4 strips cooked bacon slices, chopped

8 oz (2 cups; 226 g) cooked pasta (macaroni, elbows or curls)

2 tbsp (30 g) cold butter, chopped

Prepare a grill for direct heat and preheat it to 390°F (200°C).

To make the Crumb Topping, in a small bowl, combine the panko breadcrumbs, Parmesan cheese and Simply Delicious Seafood Rub. Set aside until needed.

Next, prepare the lobster. Brush the halved lobster tails with the olive oil. Leave the flesh in the shell so the lobster meat retains moisture. Then grill the lobster tails over high heat for 15 minutes, turning frequently or until the internal temperature reaches 130°F (55°C). Take them off the grill and set them aside, covered with foil, until needed.

Preheat a 10-inch (25-cm) cast-iron skillet directly over the fire and pour in the cream, crème fraiche, garlic, salt, pepper, all the cheese, Simply Delicious Seafood Rub and bacon. Simmer gently for 5 minutes or until the ingredients are well combined, stirring frequently.

Remove the lobster tails from their shell and chop them into small pieces. Add the lobster pieces and the cooked pasta to the sauce. Sprinkle the crumb topping over the pasta and top with the chopped butter pieces.

Now prepare a grill for indirect heat (see the Frequently Asked Grilling Questions section on page 10) and preheat it to 350°F (175°C).

Bake on the grill over indirect heat until golden brown (approximately 30 minutes). Keep warm until ready to serve.

Grilled SHRIMP PO' BOY

YIELD
4 servings

Traditionally, the shrimp in a po' boy is fried, but in our version they're grilled. We think they're juicier and tastier grilled and not fried, with a little bit of fancy added for good measure! This is one zesty and satisfying sandwich you could serve up at a BBQ party—it will be loved by all. In this recipe, we use our homemade Cajun Rub and Remoulade Sauce recipes that are delicious on seafood, chicken or beef.

CAJUN RUB

2 tbsp (14 g) smoked paprika

2 tbsp (17 g) garlic powder

2 tbsp (14 g) onion powder

1 tbsp (3 g) dried oregano

1 tbsp (5 g) ground cayenne pepper

2 tsp dried thyme

1 tbsp (18 g) salt

2 tsp (4 g) pepper

SHRIMP

1 lb (454 g) fresh or frozen shrimp, peeled, deveined and cleaned

1 tbsp (15 ml) olive oil

REMOULADE SAUCE

1 cup (240 ml) mayonnaise

1 tbsp (15 ml) French mustard

1 tbsp (9 g) finely chopped pickles

1 tbsp (4 g) finely chopped fresh parsley

1 tbsp (4 g) finely chopped fresh tarragon

2 tsp (6 g) baby capers, finely chopped

1 lemon, juiced

1 tsp hot sauce of choice

1 tsp salt

½ tsp pepper

FOR SERVING

4 medium baguette bread rolls, buttered

8 lettuce leaves

12 tomato slices

To make the Cajun Rub, in a small bowl, combine the smoked paprika, garlic powder, onion powder, dried oregano, cayenne pepper, dried thyme, salt and pepper.

Coat the shrimp with the olive oil and season them with the Cajun Rub. Cover and refrigerate for 2 hours.

To make the Remoulade Sauce, stir the mayonnaise, French mustard, pickles, parsley, tarragon, baby capers, lemon juice, hot sauce, salt and pepper until combined. Cover and refrigerate until ready to serve.

Preheat a grill for direct heat and preheat it to 390°F (200°C). Grill the shrimp on the grill grate for 3 to 4 minutes a side or until they are opaque.

Remove the shrimp from the grill and assemble the sandwiches immediately by layering the baguette with the lettuce, tomato, grilled shrimp and a teaspoon of the Remoulade Sauce.

Glazed CRISPY SKIN SALMON & MANGO SALSA

YIELD
2 servings

This recipe makes an exciting barbecue food because you have a variety of flavors that combine without losing their individual flavors. Salmon always barbecues well and has an amazing flavor with a little bit of char.

SALMON
2 tbsp (30 ml) olive oil

1 tbsp (3 g) dried oregano

1 tsp onion powder

1 tsp garlic powder

1 tsp sea salt

½ tsp black pepper

2 (7-oz [200-g]) fresh salmon fillets, 1 inch (2.5 cm) thick, skin on

1 fresh lemon, cut into wedges

DRESSING
Pulp from 1 passionfruit

1 tbsp (4 g) fresh parsley, chopped

1 tbsp (15 ml) lemon juice

2 tbsp (30 ml) balsamic vinegar

2 tbsp (30 ml) extra virgin olive oil

Pinch of sea salt

MANGO SALSA
½ mango, diced

½ cup (75 g) diced avocado

½ cup (66 g) diced cucumber

½ cup (76 g) green seedless grapes, cut into quarters

½ cup (25 g) chopped green onions

1 small chili, deseeded and chopped (optional)

GLAZE
2 tbsp (28 g) brown sugar

2 tbsp (30 ml) oyster sauce

2 tbsp (30 ml) soy sauce

1 clove garlic, crushed

To make the salmon, in a large bowl whisk the olive oil, oregano, onion powder, garlic powder, salt and pepper. Add the marinade to a large resealable plastic ziptop bag, then add the salmon. Massage the salmon so the marinade has evenly coated all the salmon pieces. Refrigerate for at least 20 minutes.

To prepare the dressing, in a large bowl mix the passionfruit pulp, parsley, lemon juice, balsamic vinegar, olive oil and salt. Set aside.

To make the Mango Salsa, in a large bowl mix the mango, avocado, cucumber, grapes, green onions and chili (if using). Refrigerate until needed. Don't add the dressing until just before you are ready to serve.

Prepare a gas or kettle grill for direct heat and preheat it to 375°F (190°C) with the lid down. You can grill directly on the grate, or you can use a barbecue hotplate. If using a hotplate, add it before preheating.

Place the salmon directly on a barbecue hotplate or grill grate, skin-side down, and cook for 5 minutes, then carefully flip the salmon with a spatula and cook an additional 3 to 4 minutes. The salmon should be nice and flaky. The internal temperature should reach 145°F (65°C). Take the salmon off the grill and let it rest for 3 minutes.

While the salmon cooks, make the glaze using a gas side burner. To a small pan over low heat, add the brown sugar, oyster sauce, soy sauce and garlic. As soon as the mixture comes to a slight boil, take it off the heat and serve it immediately with the salmon and the Mango Salsa and lemon wedges on the side.

Best GARLIC GRILLED BUTTERFLIED SHRIMP

YIELD
3 servings

Large shrimp are full of flavor and the best for barbecuing. They are quick to prepare and cook. Cleaning and marinating the shrimp the day before gives you the best results. Always start with good-quality shrimp such as king shrimp or tiger shrimp, as they have great flavor and texture especially when they are barbecued. They are a favorite of ours to serve as a side or main dish for any occasion. The garlic and herbs with the slight char from the grill bring a mild but bold flavor to the shrimp, making them even tastier. If you are a shrimp fan, you will love this recipe!

12 large raw tiger shrimp

2 tbsp (30 ml) olive oil

2 cloves garlic, crushed

¼ tsp sea salt

2 tbsp (8 g) fresh parsley, finely chopped

1 tsp fresh thyme leaves, finely chopped

½ tsp dried oregano

1 fresh lemon, cut into 4 wedges for serving

The easiest way to butterfly a shrimp is to use scissors. Start cutting along the middle of the back just under the head of the shrimp and continue right to the start of the tail. Then, using a knife, slice through the cut you have made with the scissors and butterfly the shrimp, but don't cut too deep. You want the bottom shell holding the legs to stay intact. Using your fingers, open up the shrimp like a butterfly, pressing down slowly so the shrimp stays flat. Remove the intestinal tract and discard. Rinse the shrimp then pat them dry with paper towels.

In a small bowl combine the oil, garlic, salt, parsley, thyme and oregano. With a teaspoon, fill the prawns with the marinade and set aside while you prepare the grill. The shrimp don't need to be put into the refrigerator.

Prepare a grill for direct heat and preheat it to 375°F (190°C).

Place the shrimp on the grill shell-side down and cook for 4 to 6 minutes, or until just cooked. The shrimp are ready to take off the grill when they turn opaque. Be careful not to overcook the shrimp because it will be harder to remove the meat from the shell.

Serve hot, just off the grill with a squeeze of lemon juice.

 NOTE: Keeping the shell on the shrimp while cooking adds a depth of flavor and keeps the meat moist.

Flaming SEARED OUZO SCALLOPS

YIELD
4 servings

In this recipe, we use the flambé method to impart a delicious aniseed flavor to the scallops. This recipe is influenced by our Greek heritage and brings back memories of when we traveled to Europe. Scallops are amazing when seared in a hot skillet. They don't need to be cooked for long and using the flambé method makes these a special seafood dish.

1 lb (454 g) frozen or fresh large scallops, rinsed and patted dry with paper towel

1 tbsp (15 ml) olive oil

½ tsp sea salt

3 tbsp (45 ml) ouzo

2 tbsp (28 g) butter

1 tbsp (4 g) fresh parsley, chopped (for serving)

Coat the scallops with the olive oil and season them with the salt.

Prepare a grill for direct heat and preheat it to 390°F (200°C). Place a cast-iron skillet on the grill grate and preheat it. The skillet should be hot so the scallops sizzle when they are placed in it.

Add the scallops to the preheated skillet and sear for 1 minute a side, then add the ouzo. Light the liquid with a match. There will be flames in the pan for a few seconds. When the flames are out, add the butter until it's melted and bubbling. Spoon the butter over the scallops and continue to cook for 2 to 3 minutes.

Remove the seared scallops from the skillet and serve topped with the parsley.

GRILLED OCTOPUS—*The Grill Sisters Way*

YIELD
2–4
servings

Our grilled octopus will make you feel like you're in Greece, enjoying a very special seafood delicacy. We've been grilling octopus since we were children; in fact, it was the first seafood we ever cooked and has become one of our signature dishes. Chefs around the world mostly parboil octopus prior to grilling it but to achieve that true char-grilled flavor, we believe it's important to cook it over fire the whole time. We've taught many seafood connoisseurs how to perfect the art of grilled octopus using our method and they've been thrilled with the results. You, too, can achieve tender, drool-worthy results in your own backyard.

OCTOPUS
1 lb (454 g) octopus, frozen and thawed, cleaned and tenderized (see Notes)

⅓ cup (80 ml) olive oil

1 lemon, juiced

2 cloves garlic, crushed

1 tbsp (3 g) dried oregano

¼ cup (60 ml) dry white wine

BASTING AND DRESSING MIXTURE
¼ cup (60 ml) olive oil

1 lemon, juiced

1 tsp dried oregano

½ tsp sea salt

Bring the octopus to room temperature.

To make the marinade, in a large bowl, whisk the olive oil, lemon juice, garlic, oregano and white wine until well combined. Add the octopus to the bowl and refrigerate for at least 4 hours, or overnight. When you're ready to cook, allow the octopus to reach room temperature.

To make the Basting and Dressing Mixture, in a small bowl combine the olive oil, lemon juice, oregano and salt.

Prepare a grill for direct heat and preheat it to 390°F (200°C).

Grill the octopus over direct heat for 25 to 30 minutes, with the grill lid open, turning and basting frequently with the Basting and Dressing Mixture, until the internal temperature is at least 160°F (70°C). The biggest mistake people make when grilling octopus is to remove it too soon, resulting in a texture that's too chewy. When the internal temperature reaches 160°F (70°C), test it with a metal skewer. The skewer should pierce the octopus without resistance. Remove the grilled octopus from the grill and place on a plate, covered loosely with foil, for 2 to 5 minutes. Serve drizzled with the remaining Basting and Dressing Mixture.

 NOTES: Always buy frozen octopus. Rumor has it that freezing and then thawing the octopus helps tenderize it. Marinating the octopus with an acidic ingredient such as lemon juice and/or wine also helps with the tenderizing process. The connective tissue of octopus doesn't begin to break down on the grill until the internal temperature reaches 130°F (55°C). To avoid a chewy octopus, cook it past this temperature.

Superb SHRIMP BURGER

YIELD
4 servings

From the moment you take your first bite, you'll be in seafood bliss! The flavors in this burger will tantalize your taste buds and will leave you wanting more. We prefer not to mince the shrimp too much, so there are plump chunky pieces as you dive into the seafood goodness. Need a seafood fix? This is your burger!

TARTAR SAUCE

1 cup (240 ml) mayonnaise

2 tbsp (20 g) finely chopped white onion

2 tbsp (18 g) finely chopped dill pickles

3 tbsp (26 g) capers, chopped

1 tsp lemon juice

1 tsp fresh parsley, finely chopped

Sea salt and white pepper, to taste

SHRIMP BURGERS

1.1 lb (500 g) peeled and deveined raw shrimp, finely chopped

1 lemon, juice and zest

½ cup (70 g) panko breadcrumbs

½ cup (63 g) all-purpose flour

1 tbsp (7 g) onion powder

¼ cup (60 ml) sweet chili sauce

½ cup (26 g) chopped fresh dill

½ cup (46 g) chopped fresh mint

¼ cup (12 g) thinly sliced green onions

2 cloves garlic, crushed

1 egg

1 tsp sea salt

¼ tsp pepper

2 tbsp (30 ml) olive oil

4 brioche buns

1 tbsp (14 g) butter

4 lettuce leaves

4 tomato slices

To make the Tartar Sauce, in a jar with a lid, gently mix the mayonnaise, onion, dill pickles, capers, lemon juice, parsley, salt and white pepper. Cover and refrigerate until ready to use. The Tartar Sauce can be made 1 week ahead.

To make the Shrimp Burgers, pulse the shrimp in a food processor for 5 seconds. Add the shrimp to a large bowl and mix it with the lemon juice and zest, breadcrumbs, flour, onion powder, sweet chili sauce, dill, mint, green onions, garlic, egg, salt and pepper. Divide the shrimp mixture into four equal parts. With wet hands, take one section of the shrimp mixture, roll it into a ball then flatten it slightly into a patty. Repeat this process with the rest of the mixture, then add all the patties to a plate and refrigerate to chill for 15 minutes. It is important to refrigerate the shrimp mixture so the patties will keep their shape while cooking.

Prepare a gas grill for direct heat and preheat it to 375°F (190°C). Add a barbecue hotplate and preheat for 10 minutes with the lid down.

Add the oil to the barbecue hotplate and place the shrimp patties on top. Cook them on one side for 5 minutes without flipping them. The patties should release easily. Flip the patties and cook an additional 4 minutes.

In the last few minutes of cooking, butter and grill the buns, cut-side down, to lightly toast.

Serve the shrimp burgers on the toasted buns, with one lettuce leaf, one tomato slice and the Tartar Sauce.

Crowd-Pleaser SHRIMP FRIED WONTONS

YIELD
50 wontons

These shrimp and water chestnut wontons are the perfect starter at a barbecue get-together. We use a grill side burner and fry these delicious morsels in a large wok outdoors. At Christmas time, we make hundreds of these because our friends and family always look forward to them. They're crispy, juicy and fried to perfection. Beware though, no one can ever stop at just one and that's why we make a big batch.

1.4 oz (40 g) dried shiitake mushrooms

1 lb (454 g) raw shrimp, frozen or fresh, shelled and cleaned

9 oz (250 g) green cabbage, roughly chopped

1 clove garlic, crushed

2 tbsp (30 ml) light soy sauce

1 tbsp (15 ml) sesame oil

½ cup (83 g) water chestnuts, canned, drained, chopped

1 tbsp (3 g) chopped green onions

Vegetable oil, for deep frying

50 fresh wonton wrappers

Sweet chili sauce, for serving

Using the gas side burner, add water to a small saucepan and bring it to a boil. Place the shiitake mushrooms in a heatproof bowl and cover them with the boiled water. Soak the mushrooms for 15 minutes then drain the water and set the mushrooms aside until needed.

In a food processor, pulse the shrimp, cabbage and garlic until almost smooth. Transfer the mixture to a large bowl. Stir in the soy sauce, sesame oil, water chestnuts and green onions. Combine well.

To make the wontons, place a wonton wrapper on a flat surface and add 1 teaspoon of the filling mixture to each. Bring the wrapper edges up to enclose the filling and pinch to seal the wonton, making a pouch. Repeat until all the wontons are prepared.

Using a gas grill side burner, heat the oil in a large wok or saucepan to 355°F (180°C). To check if the oil is ready for frying, add a small cube of bread into the oil. If it crisps up golden in 30 seconds, it's time to cook your wontons. When the oil is ready, deep fry the dumplings in batches for 4 to 5 minutes. You'll know the wontons are ready when they are crispy and golden in color. Serve them with the sweet chili sauce.

SUCCULENT SMOKED TROUT *with* CREAMY DILL SAUCE & TOMATO RELISH

YIELD
4 servings

This rainbow trout is full of flavor and kept succulent throughout the cook with the addition of mayonnaise. It's stuffed with fresh herbs and baked in a Traeger grill. A Traeger grill uses natural hardwood pellets to impart a delicious smoky flavor to the fish. We've used apple pellets in the Traeger grill. A gas grill or charcoal kettle can also be used for this recipe. Apple wood chips can be used in a smoke box for a gas grill and they can be placed directly on charcoal in a charcoal kettle.

TROUT
1 (1.7-lb [800-g]) whole fresh rainbow trout, cleaned

1 tbsp (15 ml) olive oil

1 tsp salt

1 tsp cracked pepper

2 tbsp (30 ml) mayonnaise

6 thin lemon slices + wedges to serve

1 small bunch fresh parsley

1 small bunch fresh dill

CREAMY DILL SAUCE
½ cup (120 ml) Greek-style yogurt

½ cup (120 ml) sour cream

1 tbsp (15 ml) horseradish cream

¼ cup (13 g) fresh dill, chopped

1 tbsp (3 g) chopped fresh chives

½ tsp salt

¼ tsp pepper

TOMATO RELISH
1 tsp sugar

2 tbsp (30 ml) lemon juice

1 medium tomato, finely chopped

1 small Spanish onion, finely chopped

2 tbsp (6 g) chopped fresh mint

½ tsp salt

¼ tsp pepper

Rinse the trout under cold water (including the cavity) and pat it dry with paper towels. Make three diagonal slits, ½ inch (1 cm) deep on each side of the thickest part of the fish. This helps impart flavors into the flesh during grilling.

Coat the fish with the olive oil and season it with the salt and pepper. Add the mayonnaise, lemon slices, parsley and dill to the cavity of the fish. The mayonnaise will help keep the flesh succulent throughout the smoking process.

To make the Creamy Dill Sauce, in a small bowl, mix the Greek yogurt, sour cream, horseradish cream, dill, chives, salt and pepper. Refrigerate until needed.

For the Tomato Relish, in another small bowl, mix the sugar and lemon juice until slightly dissolved. Then add the tomato, onion, mint, salt and pepper. Refrigerate until needed.

Prepare a smoker grill for indirect heat (see the Frequently Asked Grilling Questions section on page 10) and set it to 350°F (180°C). If you're using a gas grill, add a smoker box filled with pre-smoked apple chips. For a kettle grill, add a handful of apple chips directly to the lit charcoal.

Place the fish on the grill grate in the smoker and cook for 10 minutes a side, or until the fish is cooked through. The fish should flake easily and without resistance away from the bone with a fork when it's ready. The internal temperature should be approximately 145°F (65°C).

Serve immediately with the Creamy Dill Sauce and Tomato Relish on the side.

Spectacular SALADS

In this chapter, we have included our most spectacular salads that are tasty side dishes to complete your barbecue feast. These are salads that are full of flavor, quick to make and are suited to be served alongside any barbecued meat, seafood or poultry. When you combine char-grilled meats or seafood cooked hot and fast with fresh, crisp salad, the combination is unforgettable. These salads can also be stand-alone meals.

Our Amazing Greek Goddess Salad with Grilled Olives (page 124) is like no other! We use the combination of Kalamata olives with char-grilled green olives for a flavor-packed deliciousness.

This chapter includes our recipes for Grilled Spicy Thai Beef Salad (page 116), Fresh & Delicious Tabouli Fattoush Salad (page 119), BBQ Shrimp & Calamari Salad (page 120), Colorful Quinoa & Tofu Salad with Almond Vinaigrette (page 127) and more.

Grilled SPICY THAI BEEF SALAD

YIELD
4 servings

In this recipe, thick and juicy flank steak is grilled to perfection and then added to a fresh herb and cucumber salad that has a spicy kick. We've created a tangy and refreshing dressing that has an Asian influence to drizzle over the beef salad. This is the perfect summer salad to serve as a starter or as a main at your next barbecue party.

STEAK
1 (1½-lb [600-g]) flank steak

1 tbsp (15 ml) avocado oil

1 tsp salt

1 tsp pepper

DRESSING
1 tbsp (15 ml) avocado oil

2 tbsp (30 ml) soy sauce

1 tsp sesame oil

2 tbsp (30 ml) apple cider vinegar

1 fresh lime, juiced

1 tbsp (15 ml) honey

½ long red chili, sliced finely

½ tsp cayenne pepper (optional)

2 cloves garlic, crushed

2 tbsp (12 g) finely chopped ginger

2 tbsp (2 g) finely chopped cilantro

SALAD
1 cup (92 g) fresh mint leaves, rinsed and chopped

1 cup (17 g) cilantro leaves, rinsed and chopped + 1 tablespoon (1 g) for serving

1 cup (28 g) mixed salad leaves, rinsed and torn

1 large cucumber, sliced thinly

2–3 shallots, thinly sliced

1 Thai chili, thinly sliced (optional)

1 tbsp (4 g) finely chopped fresh lemongrass (optional)

Coat the flank steak with the avocado oil and season with salt and pepper. Allow the steak to reach room temperature.

To make the dressing, in a medium bowl, whisk the avocado oil, soy sauce, sesame oil, apple cider vinegar, lime juice, honey, chili, cayenne pepper, garlic, ginger and cilantro until well combined. Set aside until needed.

Prepare a grill for direct heat and preheat it to 390°F (200°C). Grill the flank steak for 4 to 5 minutes per side (for medium rare) or until cooked to your liking. Remove the steak from the heat and let it rest for 5 to 10 minutes before slicing thinly across the grain.

In a serving bowl, combine the mint, 1 cup (17 g) of the cilantro, salad greens, cucumber, shallots, chili and lemongrass (if using) then add the grilled flank steak on top. Drizzle the salad with the dressing and gently toss before serving with the additional 1 tablespoon (1 g) of cilantro.

Fresh & Delicious
TABOULI FATTOUSH SALAD

YIELD
6–8
servings

Tabouli is a refreshing and tangy salad made of soaked bulgur wheat or quinoa and plenty of fresh lemon juice, parsley, mint and green onions. The toasted pita bread gives a nice crunch to this herby salad. We also add a ground spice called sumac, which comes from a dried purple berry, to add a sour fruity flavor to the dressing and complement the tabouli salad. This salad makes an excellent accompaniment to any grilled steak, chicken or seafood.

½ cup (88 g) dry fine bulgur wheat (or 1 cup [185 g] cooked quinoa)

½ cup (120 ml) fresh lemon juice

¼ cup + 3 tbsp (105 ml) extra virgin olive oil, divided

½ tsp sea salt

1 tsp sumac

3 cups (180 g) fresh parsley, finely chopped

1 cup (92 g) fresh mint, finely chopped

2 large tomatoes, finely chopped

2 Lebanese cucumbers, finely chopped

4 green onions, finely chopped

1 small red onion, finely chopped

1 tsp dried mint

3 large pita breads

To prepare the bulgur wheat, place the bulgur wheat in a medium bowl and cover completely by ½-inch (1-cm) of hot water. Let the bulgur absorb the water and soften. This will take approximately 15 minutes.

Meanwhile, in a small bowl, whisk the lemon juice, ¼ cup (60 ml) of the olive oil, salt and sumac.

When the bulgur is softened, add it to a large bowl with the parsley, mint, tomatoes, cucumber, green onions, onion and dried mint. Add the dressing (see note) and refrigerate for 20 minutes so all the flavors can combine.

Meanwhile, prepare a grill for direct heat and preheat it to 375°F (190°C). Brush the pita breads with the remaining 3 tbsp (45 ml) of olive oil and place them on the grill. Toast both sides of the pita bread for 10 to 20 seconds. Once off the grill, use your hands to break up the bread into small pieces and add them to the top of the tabouli salad (see note) and serve.

 NOTE: The tabouli salad can last up to 4 days in the refrigerator without the dressing or pita bread pieces. Add the dressing and pita bread right before you would like to serve this salad.

BBQ SHRIMP & CALAMARI SALAD

YIELD
4 servings

This salad has an incredible char-grilled flavor and includes our favorite seafood dressing. It's a seafood salad that you can enjoy all year and it's quick to make. Shrimp and calamari don't take long on the grill, which makes this salad ideal any day of a busy week. The dressing and salad greens can be prepared ahead of time, then tossed with the grilled seafood right before serving. This delightfully grilled seafood salad is sure to impress your friends and family.

SEAFOOD

¼ lb (113 g; 4 to 6) calamari bodies (including tentacles), cleaned and patted dry

24 large raw, fresh or frozen shrimp, peeled, deveined and heads removed

2 tbsp (30 ml) olive oil

1 lemon, juiced

½ tsp dried oregano

SEAFOOD DRESSING

½ cup (120 ml) olive oil

¼ cup (60 ml) white wine vinegar

1 lemon, juiced

1 tsp French mustard

1 tbsp (8 g) baby capers, chopped

1 tsp dried oregano

1 tbsp (4 g) chopped fresh parsley

½ tsp salt

¼ tsp pepper

1 clove garlic, optional

SALAD

5 cups (142 g) mixed salad greens

1 medium cucumber, sliced

2 tbsp (7 g) Spanish onion, thinly sliced

1 tbsp (4 g) chopped fresh flat-leaf parsley

1 tbsp (2 g) chopped fresh mint

Cut the calamari rings ½-inch (1-cm) wide. Place the shrimp and calamari in a large bowl. In a small bowl, whisk the olive oil, lemon juice and dried oregano until combined. Pour the mixture over the seafood. Toss to coat the seafood well.

Prepare a grill for direct heat and preheat it to 390°F (200°C).

Grill the seafood in batches, hot and fast, starting with the shrimp for 3 minutes a side or until they are opaque. Follow with the calamari for 2 to 4 minutes a side and make sure you don't overcook any of the seafood or it will become rubbery.

To make the Seafood Dressing, in a medium bowl, whisk the olive oil, white wine vinegar, lemon juice, mustard, capers, oregano, parsley, salt, pepper and garlic (if using).

In a large serving bowl, arrange the salad leaves, cucumber, onion, parsley and mint. Place the grilled seafood on the salad, garnish with lemon wedges, and drizzle with the Seafood Dressing.

Grilled CHICKEN CAESAR SALAD

YIELD
4 servings

When we combine our tasty grilled chicken with tangy dressing, grilled garlic sourdough croutons and the classic Romaine, it is a true flavor explosion. This salad has always been a winner at our barbecue parties as a starter or main and is guaranteed to impress your friends and family. The Garlic Croutons, Caesar Dressing and chicken marinade can all be made ahead of time to make this recipe even quicker.

CHICKEN

3 cloves garlic, crushed

2 tbsp (30 ml) fresh lemon juice

1 tsp dried oregano

3 tbsp (45 ml) olive oil

1 tsp sea salt

¼ tsp pepper

2 large chicken breasts, skinless

CAESAR DRESSING

½ cup (120 ml) mayonnaise

½ cup (120 ml) sour cream

2 cloves garlic, crushed

4 anchovies, packed in oil

1 tsp Dijon mustard

2 tbsp (30 ml) fresh lemon juice

1 tsp Worcestershire sauce

¼ cup (25 g) grated Parmesan cheese

¼ tsp sea salt

¼ tsp pepper

GARLIC CROUTONS

2 tbsp (30 ml) olive oil

2 cloves garlic, crushed

¼ tsp fresh parsley, finely chopped

¼ tsp salt

2 cups (70 g) ½-inch (1-cm) cubes sourdough bread

6 cups (200 g) Romaine lettuce, roughly chopped

¼ cup (25 g) shaved Parmesan cheese

To make the chicken, in a small bowl, mix the garlic, lemon juice, oregano, olive oil, salt and pepper. Add the chicken breasts and rub the marinade all over both sides. Let the chicken sit in the marinade in the refrigerator for an hour, or overnight.

For the Caesar Dressing, use a food processor to blend the mayonnaise, sour cream, garlic, anchovies, Dijon mustard, lemon juice, Worcestershire sauce, Parmesan cheese, salt and pepper until everything has combined into a smooth dressing. Refrigerate until needed.

Prepare a grill for direct heat with a grill grate and a hotplate and preheat it to 375°F (190°C).

To make the Garlic Croutons, in a large bowl, mix the olive oil, garlic, parsley and salt. Add the sourdough cubes to the bowl and toss to coat them well, then place them on the preheated hotplate. Keep turning the cubes as they will toast up quickly within 3 minutes. Once toasted, set aside.

Add the chicken breast to the grill grate and cook for approximately 5 minutes per side. Take the chicken breast off the grill when the internal temperature reaches 165°F (75°C). Let the chicken rest for 5 minutes then cut it into ½-inch (1-cm) slices.

To a large serving bowl, add the lettuce and drizzle with the dressing. Add the grilled chicken slices and top with the Garlic Croutons and the shaved Parmesan cheese to serve.

AMAZING GREEK GODDESS SALAD *with* GRILLED OLIVES

YIELD
4 servings

Once you try our Greek Goddess salad, it will become one of your go-to favorites. We have added dill and oregano, giving an extra freshness to this traditional salad. The zesty juices from the lemon and cherry tomatoes, and the saltiness from the feta cheese and Kalamata olives give another layer of flavor. Using a good extra virgin olive oil makes a big difference as well. We also love dipping a piece of crusty bread to soak up the dressing. It's a salad that not only looks beautiful and colourful but tastes amazing too.

DRESSING

¼ cup (60 ml) extra virgin olive oil

1 tbsp (15 ml) lemon juice

2 tbsp (30 ml) red wine vinegar

1 tsp dried oregano

¼ tsp sea salt

SALAD

1 heart (head) Romaine lettuce

1 large cucumber, cut in half lengthwise, then sliced into ¼-inch (6-mm) half-moons

2 cups (298 g) cherry tomatoes, halved

1 red bell pepper, deseeded and sliced

1 small red onion, sliced thinly

½ cup (72 g) pitted Kalamata olives

3 oz (85 g) block of feta

1 tbsp (3 g) fresh dill, chopped

2 tbsp (7 g) fresh oregano, chopped

GRILLED OLIVES

½ cup (90 g) mixed olives, pitted (mixed varieties)

2 tsp (10 ml) olive oil

To make the dressing, in a small bowl, whisk the olive oil, lemon juice, red wine vinegar, oregano and salt until well combined. Set aside.

Separate the lettuce leaves and thoroughly wash and dry them with paper towels. Chop the leaves and place them in a large bowl. Add the cucumber, cherry tomatoes, bell pepper, onion and Kalamata olives. Top the salad with the block of feta cheese, dill and oregano, then drizzle the dressing all over the salad.

To prepare the grilled olives, thread them onto metal skewers and brush them with the olive oil.

Prepare a grill for direct heat and preheat it to 390°F (200°C). Cook the skewered olives on the grill grate for 2 minutes in total, turning frequently or until the skin blisters slightly. Remove the skewered olives from the grill and serve them on top of this Amazing Greek Goddess Salad.

COLORFUL QUINOA & TOFU SALAD *with* ALMOND VINAIGRETTE

YIELD
3 servings

This standout salad can be prepared ahead of time and is crisp, fresh and packed full of flavor. We like to use firm, non-silken tofu for grilling as it takes on our balsamic marinade well. Be prepared to get lots of requests for this salad. It's a winning combination!

QUINOA
1 cup (170 g) quinoa
2 cups (480 ml) water
½ tsp sea salt

GRILLED BALSAMIC TOFU
1 (14-oz [397-g]) block firm tofu
1 tbsp (15 ml) olive oil
¼ cup (60 ml) balsamic vinegar
2 cloves garlic, minced
1 tbsp (15 ml) maple syrup
Salt and pepper, to taste

ALMOND VINAIGRETTE
¼ cup (54 g) slivered almonds
¼ cup (60 ml) extra virgin olive oil
1 tsp honey
2 tbsp (30 ml) fresh lemon juice
3 tbsp (45 ml) white balsamic vinegar or white wine vinegar
½ tsp sea salt

QUINOA SALAD
1 cup (42 g) baby arugula, chopped
¼ cup (24 g) shredded coconut
½ cup (76 g) quartered white seedless grapes
½ cup (35 g) thinly sliced red cabbage
1 cup (132 g) diced cucumber
½ cup (25 g) chopped green onions
½ cup (75 g) chopped orange bell pepper
½ cup (75 g) chopped red bell pepper
½ cup (50 g) pomegranate seeds
¼ cup (39 g) corn kernels, cooked

Rinse the quinoa in a fine mesh strainer under cold water for a minute. Using a gas side burner, combine the quinoa, water and salt in a medium saucepan and bring to a boil. Lower the heat to a simmer with the lid on for 15 minutes. Turn off the heat and let it sit with the lid on for 10 minutes. Remove the quinoa from the pot, fluff it with a fork and place it into a bowl to cool.

Meanwhile, prepare the tofu. Drain the tofu and pat it dry with paper towels. Cut the tofu into 1–inch (2.5–cm) thick slices and set aside.

In a medium bowl, whisk the olive oil, balsamic vinegar, garlic, maple syrup, salt and pepper until well combined. Add the tofu to the bowl and coat it well with the marinade. Set the tofu and marinade aside for 15 minutes. Tofu doesn't need to marinate for a long time as flavors soak into it quickly.

While the tofu marinates, make the Almond Vinaigrette. In a large bowl, whisk the almonds, olive oil, honey, lemon juice, white balsamic vinegar and sea salt. To the same bowl, add the quinoa and mix in the baby arugula, coconut, grapes, cabbage, cucumber, green onions, orange bell pepper, red bell pepper, pomegranate and corn.

Prepare a grill for direct heat and preheat it to 390°F (200°C). Remove the tofu from the marinade and place the slices on the grill grate. Cook the tofu for 5 to 7 minutes a side, using a metal spatula to flip it over. Serve the grilled balsamic tofu on top of the quinoa salad.

Brilliant POTATO & BACON BBQ SALAD

YIELD
4 servings

Two favourite foods put together make for a very tempting combination. Our families just love potatoes, crispy bacon and barbecue, so we have combined them in this scrumptious Brilliant Potato & Bacon BBQ Salad. The flavors are so tasty whether eaten hot or cold. This is, without a doubt, the best potato and bacon BBQ salad you'll ever make.

POTATOES
lb (500 g) baby potatoes, washed

1½ tsp (9 g) sea salt, divided

¼ tsp black pepper

2 cloves garlic, crushed

¼ cup (60 ml) olive oil

3 bacon slices, chopped

DRESSING
2 tbsp (30 ml) olive oil

½ small red onion, finely diced

2 tbsp (30 ml) fresh lemon juice

1 tsp seeded mustard

2 tbsp (6 g) finely chopped chives

2 tbsp (8 g) finely chopped fresh parsley

½ tsp sea salt

Using a gas side burner, place the baby potatoes in a large pot of cold water and add 1 teaspoon of salt. Bring the potatoes to a boil then simmer for 7 minutes until the potatoes are tender. Rinse the potatoes under cold water, leaving the skin on. Cut the potatoes in half.

In a small bowl, mix the remaining ½ teaspoon of salt, pepper, garlic and olive oil then pour the mixture over the potatoes and toss gently to coat them well. Let the potatoes sit for 15 minutes to absorb the flavors.

Prepare a grill for direct heat and preheat it to 390°F (200°C).

Place the marinated potatoes on the grill grate and grill them for about 4 minutes per side until you have nice grill marks, then take the potatoes off the grill and set aside.

Grill the bacon for 2 to 3 minutes per side, or until crispy. Remove the bacon from the grill and slice into ½-inch (1-cm) squares. Set aside to cool.

To make the dressing, whisk the olive oil, red onion, lemon juice, seeded mustard, chives, parsley and salt.

Add the grilled potatoes and bacon to a large bowl. Pour the dressing over the grilled potatoes and crispy bacon, toss and serve.

Vibrant
VEGETARIAN &
SIDE DISHES

We believe every great BBQ book should have a chapter on grilled vegetarian meals and special sides. That's why we created the vibrant and tasty recipes in this chapter.

When vegetables are char-grilled, the smoky flavors really enhance them, making for a great side or main vegetarian meal. They can be cooking on the side grill or burner while you grill the main course.

And, believe it or not, you can grill cheese! Halloumi cheese is wonderful to barbecue as it has a firm texture that doesn't melt when grilled. Try it in our BBQ Halloumi & Veggie Skewers with Garlic Aioli (page 136). In this chapter, you will also find fabulous falafels (page 132), mouthwatering Mexican street corn (page 143), the easiest rice pilaf (page 148) and more.

Our vegetarian barbecue recipes taste so good, even die-hard carnivores will love them!

FABULOUS FALAFELS *with* HOMEMADE HUMMUS & CARAMELIZED ONIONS

YIELD
4 servings
(4 pieces
per serving)

These falafels are a great vegetarian snack or main dish. They are light, fluffy and full of flavor. The aroma of the herbs and spices is so fragrant. They make great lunchbox additions that can be eaten hot or cold and they even freeze well.

FALAFELS

1 cup (200 g) dried chickpeas soaked in water overnight (don't use canned; see Notes)

1 cup (60 g) fresh parsley, roughly chopped

1 cup (16 g) fresh cilantro, roughly chopped, with stems

1 cup (92 g) fresh mint, roughly chopped

1 large onion, chopped

1½ cups (75 g) chopped green onions

3 cloves garlic, chopped

½ tsp baking powder

¼ cup (31 g) all-purpose flour

1 tbsp (5 g) cumin

1 tbsp (5 g) ground coriander

1 tsp sweet paprika

1 tsp sea salt

¼ cup (60 ml) water

1 cup (240 ml) light olive oil, for shallow frying

4 pita breads, for serving

To make the falafels, place the soaked chickpeas, parsley, cilantro, mint, onion, green onions, garlic, baking powder, flour, cumin, coriander, sweet paprika, sea salt and water into a food processor. Process until the mixture forms a firm paste-like consistency.

Using a tablespoon, scoop up some of the mixture (it should be about the size of a walnut) and, with both hands, roll it into a ball then flatten it slightly. Repeat until all the mixture is used. Place the balls on a dish and refrigerate for 30 minutes.

(continued)

HUMMUS

¾ cup (123 g) canned chickpeas (or dried chickpeas soaked in water overnight), reserve a few for garnish

2 lemons, juiced

2 cloves garlic, crushed

2½ tbsp (37 ml) olive oil, divided

⅔ cup (160 ml) tahini paste

½ tsp ground cumin

½ tsp sea salt

Pinch of sweet paprika

½ tbsp (1 g) fresh parsley, chopped

CARAMELIZED ONIONS

2 tbsp (30 ml) olive oil

2 large yellow onions, sliced

Pinch of sea salt

2 tbsp (30 ml) Worcestershire sauce

Meanwhile, to make the hummus, add the canned or pre-soaked chickpeas, lemon juice, garlic, 2 tablespoons (30 ml) of the olive oil, tahini, cumin and salt into a food processor. Process until smooth and creamy. Sprinkle with the sweet paprika, reserved chickpeas, parsley and remaining ½ tablespoon (7 ml) of olive oil to garnish.

Prepare a gas or kettle grill for direct heat using a grill grate and a hotplate and preheat it to 375°F (190°C) with the lid down. Have a plate with a layer of paper towels on hand.

To cook the falafels, place a cast-iron skillet on the grill and add the olive oil. Working in batches, add some falafels to the skillet, without overcrowding. Cook for 3 to 4 minutes per side until nice and golden, then remove. Place the cooked falafels on the paper towel–lined plate to remove any excess oil. Continue until all falafels are cooked.

To make the caramelized onions, add the olive oil, onions and salt to the hotplate. Cook for 8 minutes, continuously stirring. Add the Worcestershire sauce as the onions begin to sweat then cook for an additional 4 minutes, or until the onions are caramelized.

Serve the falafels with the hummus, caramelized onions and pita bread.

NOTES: For the falafel mixture, only use dried chickpeas but for the hummus, canned chickpeas are fine. We don't recommend using canned chickpeas because they don't hold their form and become very crumbly. We find that using pre-soaked chickpeas works better when making falafels.

This mixture can be made a day ahead and stored in the fridge until you're ready to form and fry the falafel patties.

BBQ HALLOUMI & VEGGIE SKEWERS *with* GARLIC AIOLI

YIELD
4 servings
(2 skewers
per serving)

These skewers are loved by vegetarians and carnivores alike! Halloumi cheese has a deliciously salty flavor and is amazing to grill because it has a firm texture that can withstand high heat well. For our bright and colorful halloumi and veggie skewers, we use the grill grate so they're perfectly charred with a smoky flavor and then we serve them with a quick and creamy garlic aioli.

GARLIC AIOLI

1 cup (240 ml) mayonnaise

3 cloves garlic, minced

3 tbsp (45 ml) lemon juice

Salt and pepper, to taste

HALLOUMI & VEGGIE SKEWERS

½ lb (226 g) halloumi, patted dry and cut into 1-inch (2.5-cm) squares

1 medium zucchini, chopped into ½-inch (1.25-cm) rounds

1 medium orange bell pepper, cut into 1-inch (2.5-cm) squares

1 medium red bell pepper, cut into 1-inch (2.5-cm) squares

1 medium yellow bell pepper, cut into 1-inch (2.5-cm) squares

1 medium Spanish onion, cut into thin wedges

Olive oil, for brushing

8 metal skewers

Lemon wedges to serve (optional)

Prepare a grill for direct heat and preheat it to 390°F (200°C).

To make the Garlic Aioli, in a small bowl mix the mayonnaise, garlic, lemon juice, salt and pepper. Refrigerate until needed.

To make the skewers, thread alternating pieces of halloumi and vegetables onto the skewers and brush them with olive oil. We like to thread 2 pieces of halloumi and 9 pieces of vegetables per skewer.

Cook the skewers on the grill grate, over direct heat, for 10 minutes, turning frequently until cooked through and evenly.

Squeeze lemon juice over the halloumi cheese and veggie skewers and sprinkle with cilantro before serving, if desired. Serve with the Garlic Aioli on the side.

Cheesy JALAPEÑO DAMPER

YIELD
4–6
servings

This hot, soft and cheesy bread with a surprise spicy kick, straight out of a Dutch oven brings back memories for us. Growing up, we'd walk to a bakery close to our house every morning with our two younger sisters and buy piping hot fresh bread. Damper in Australia is a traditional bread cooked in a Dutch oven. We make this damper in our kettle grill, using charcoal. These days, we love making it in our Dutch oven as we sit around the fire and spend quality time with our families. Make sure you have butter on hand, ready to slather on the hot damper when it's ready.

3 cups (375 g) self-rising flour

1 cup (113 g) grated sharp Cheddar cheese

1 cup (240 ml) milk

2 tbsp (30 ml) heavy cream

1 tbsp (15 g) sugar

1 tsp salt

1 tbsp (6 g) dried mixed herbs

1 jalapeño, thinly sliced

½ stick (55 g) butter, softened, plus extra for serving

Line a Dutch oven or baking tray with parchment paper.

Prepare a charcoal grill kettle for indirect heat (see the Frequently Asked Grilling Questions section on page 10) and preheat it to 350°F (180°C). The lit charcoal will be on one side of the grill and the Dutch oven or baking tray will be placed opposite it. To prevent the bottom of the damper from burning, if using a Dutch oven, place a trivet on the indirect heat side of the grill grate.

In a large bowl, mix the flour, Cheddar cheese, milk, cream, sugar, salt, herbs and jalapeño. Add the butter and rub it into the mixture with your hands. Knead the mixture until a smooth dough forms. Shape the dough into a round loaf and cut a cross into the top.

Place the round dough on the trivet in the Dutch oven or on the parchment-lined baking tray on the indirect heat side of the grill, opposite the lit charcoal. Place 15 pieces of charcoal on top of the Dutch oven if it has a cast-iron lid. Close the lid.

Bake the bread for 50 to 60 minutes, or until it is golden brown. You can also insert a metal skewer or sharp knife in the thickest part of the damper to see if it's ready. It is done if the skewer comes out clean, with no batter stuck to it. Serve with plenty of butter.

GRILLED RAINBOW VEGGIES *with* HERB VINAIGRETTE

YIELD
4–6
servings

Char-grilled veggies make a meal on their own or are delicious served as a colorful Mediterranean-style side. Marinating the veggies before grilling them makes all the difference. Finishing them off with a honey and herb vinaigrette makes a great accompaniment to the natural sweetness of the vegetables. These grilled veggies are also a favorite with the kids. They are delicious eaten cold or added to lunch boxes.

VEGETABLES

4 tbsp (60 ml) olive oil

2 cloves garlic, minced

1 tsp dried oregano

1 tsp sea salt

¼ tsp pepper

2 ears sweet corn, husks removed and cut into fourths

2 small zucchini, halved lengthways

6 small mushrooms, any variety

1 red bell pepper, seeded and cut into quarters

1 yellow bell pepper, seeded and cut into quarters

2 red onions, cut into 8 wedges

6 Brussels sprouts

4 (¾-inch [2-cm]) wedges of pumpkin (any variety), skin on

2 beets, cut in quarters

8 spears asparagus

HERB VINAIGRETTE

1 tsp honey

2 tbsp (30 ml) balsamic vinegar

1 tbsp (3 g) fresh oregano, chopped

1 tbsp (4 g) fresh parsley, chopped

2 tbsp (30 ml) extra virgin olive oil

1 tbsp (15 ml) fresh lemon juice

½ tsp sea salt

Prepare a gas or kettle grill for direct heat and preheat it to 375°F (190°C) with the lid down.

To make the marinade for the vegetables, in a large bowl whisk the olive oil, garlic, oregano, salt and pepper until well combined. Add the corn, zucchini, mushrooms, red bell pepper, yellow bell pepper, onions, Brussels sprouts, pumpkin, beet and asparagus and coat the vegetables well with the marinade.

Place all the vegetables directly on the grill grate and cook the corn, zucchini, mushrooms, bell peppers, onions and asparagus for 5 to 7 minutes per side. The Brussels sprouts, pumpkin and beets will require 10 to 15 minutes a side.

As the vegetables are cooking, prepare the Herb Vinaigrette. In a small bowl, whisk the honey, balsamic vinegar, oregano, parsley, olive oil, lemon juice and salt.

Drizzle the grilled vegetables with the Herb Vinaigrette and serve.

CHAR-GRILLED MEXICAN STREET CORN *with* SRIRACHA SAUCE

YIELD
4 servings

When you are looking for an easy yet tasty side dish, this Char-Grilled Mexican Street Corn is the one. The sweetness from the corn and the spicy touch from the Sriracha Sauce make it a perfect side next to any barbecued meat or even as a standalone side. When you think of Mexico, you think colorful, flavorful and spicy, and that is what you get with this delicious recipe.

MEXICAN STREET CORN
4 sweet corn cobs
2 tbsp (30 ml) olive oil
2 tbsp (30 ml) melted butter
1 tsp onion powder
¼ tsp sweet paprika
¼ tsp sea salt
2 tbsp (2 g) finely chopped fresh cilantro

SRIRACHA SAUCE
¾ cup (180 ml) mayonnaise
2 tbsp (30 ml) sriracha
1 tbsp (15 ml) honey
1 clove garlic, minced
2 tbsp (30 ml) fresh lime juice
Sea salt, to taste

Prepare a grill for direct heat and preheat it to 375°F (190°C).

Peel back the husks from each corn cob without tearing them and remove the silk. Tie kitchen twine around the pulled-back husk to form a handle.

Brush the corn evenly all over with the olive oil and place the ears on the hot grill. Grill the corn for approximately 12 minutes, turning occasionally, so the corn is cooked evenly and has some charred kernels. You'll know when the corn is ready if a pierced kernel is tender.

To make the Sriracha Sauce, in a small bowl, mix the mayonnaise, sriracha, honey, garlic, lime juice and salt until well combined. Set aside until needed.

While the corn is cooking, melt the butter in a small bowl, then add the onion powder, sweet paprika and salt. When the corn is removed from the grill, brush the butter mixture all over the corn. Place the buttered corn on a plate and add a little of the Sriracha Sauce on top, then sprinkle with the cilantro.

CHEESE & CHIVE CREAMY DOUBLE BAKED POTATO

YIELD
4 servings

These double baked cheese and chive jacket potatoes are creamy, tasty and glorious to eat all year round. We love potatoes, and stuffing them with creamy mashed potatoes and cheese makes them an amazing side dish or dinner with an accompanying salad.

4 large baking potatoes

2 tbsp (30 ml) olive oil

1 tsp salt

1½ cups (170 g) grated Cheddar cheese, divided

5 tbsp (75 ml) sour cream, plus extra for serving

2 tbsp (30 ml) milk

1 stick butter (113 g), softened

2 tbsp (3 g) chopped chives, plus extra for serving

½ tsp pepper

Prepare a grill for indirect heat (see the Frequently Asked Grilling Questions section on page 10) and preheat it to 350°F (180°C).

Use a fork to pierce holes in each potato. This will allow the steam to escape and prevent them from exploding in the grill. Brush them with olive oil and season with the salt. Wrap each potato in foil and place them on the grill, using indirect heat with the lid closed. Bake for 60 minutes, rotating the potato midway. They will be soft when they're ready and a knife will pierce them without resistance.

Remove the potatoes from the grill, and when they're cool enough to handle, remove the foil and cut the potatoes open at the top. Scoop out one third of the flesh from each potato and place it in a bowl. Mash the potato flesh then stir in 1 cup (113 g) of the cheese, the sour cream, milk, butter, chives and pepper. Add the mashed mixture back into the potatoes and then each potato with the remaining ½ cup (57 g) of the cheese.

Make four foil boats for the potatoes to sit in. To make the boat, use a piece of foil that is double the length of your potato. Fold it in half so you've got a double layer and place the potato in the center. Fold in the sides half-way up the potato to form a boat. Repeat with the remaining potatoes. The foil boats will help prevent the potatoes from drying out and burning. Return the potatoes in their boats to the grill. Bake them again for 20 to 25 minutes or until the cheese on top is melted and slightly golden.

Serve the potatoes hot with sour cream and chopped chives.

CHAR-GRILLED BELL PEPPERS *with* WALNUTS, FETA & HONEY DRESSING

YIELD
4 servings

In this recipe, the sweetness of grilled bell peppers and honey garlic dressing combined with the salty feta cheese and walnuts is heavenly. When bell peppers are grilled, they release an abundance of sweetness. Grilling bell peppers always brings back fond childhood memories of when we would help our mother place the bell peppers on the griddle and turn them as they charred on each side. In most homes in Greece, you will find a plate of grilled bell peppers with olive oil and garlic in the fridge. It is one of those simple dishes that you can have on its own, on bread or as a side dish.

HONEY AND GARLIC DRESSING

1 tsp honey

2 cloves garlic, finely chopped

2 tbsp (30 ml) balsamic vinegar

1 tbsp (8 g) fresh parsley, finely chopped

4 tbsp (60 ml) extra virgin olive oil, divided

BELL PEPPER SALAD

2 red bell peppers

2 yellow bell peppers

2 green bell peppers

4 oz (113 g) baby arugula, for serving

⅓ cup (50 g) crumbled feta cheese

¼ cup (28 g) coarsely chopped roasted walnut pieces

To make the dressing, in a small bowl, combine the honey, garlic, balsamic vinegar, parsley and 3 tablespoons (45 ml) of the olive oil.

Prepare a grill for direct heat and preheat it to 375°F (190°C).

Brush the bell peppers with the remaining 1 tablespoon (15 ml) of the olive oil and place them on the grill, whole, until they start to char and blister all around. It will take approximately 3 minutes per side. Keeping the bell peppers whole makes them easier to handle on the grill with metal tongs.

Remove the bell peppers from the grill and place them into a plastic ziptop bag and let them sit for 30 minutes. The bell peppers will become soft and the skin, stem and seeds will be easier to remove. Peel and core the peppers and remove the seeds. Tear the peppers into strips.

Scatter the arugula on a plate, then place the bell pepper strips on top. Drizzle the dressing, feta cheese and walnuts on top.

No Fail Quick & Easy
15 MINUTE RICE PILAF

YIELD
6 servings

This quick and easy rice pilaf was one of the first sides we learned how to cook as children. We didn't have a lot of money growing up and our meals were simple yet deliciously nutritious. Traditionally, pilaf includes onion, but in our recipe it's optional. Using white, long grain, jasmine or basmati rice provides a perfectly fluffy result while helping retain nutrients. We like to use our grill side burner and prepare the rice while we grill our protein. In this recipe, we use chicken stock powder but you could also use beef, vegetable or your favorite barbecue rub for flavor.

2 cups (400 g) uncooked white rice, long grain, jasmine or basmati

2 tbsp (30 ml) olive oil

1 small onion, finely diced (optional)

3 tsp (10 g) chicken stock powder

½ tsp cayenne pepper (optional)

½ tsp cumin (optional)

½ tsp sweet paprika (optional)

4 cups (960 ml) water

Rinse the rice with cold water until the water runs clear.

Using a gas grill side burner, warm the olive oil in a medium saucepan over low heat then add the onion, if using, and sauté for 3 minutes. Add the rice, chicken stock powder and, if using, the cayenne pepper, cumin and sweet paprika, stirring frequently. Slightly toast the rice for 2 to 3 minutes until it is fragrant and well coated in the oil and chicken stock powder and spices (if using).

Pour the water into the saucepan and increase the heat to medium. When it's simmering, reduce the heat to low and cover the pot. Set a timer for 15 minutes and allow the rice pilaf to cook. It's important that you don't remove the saucepan lid during the cook because heat and steam will escape, which leads to the rice not cooking evenly and becoming mushy.

Remove the saucepan from the heat and let the rice sit for at least 10 minutes (no peeking!). When you're ready to serve, fluff the rice with a fork and transfer it to a bowl.

Dreamy DESSERTS

Every good barbecue needs a delectable and dreamy dessert to finish a delicious meal. The desserts we've created can be cooked using a gas grill, charcoal or a pellet grill smoker and taste divine.

You will be surprised at the variety of desserts you can cook on your barbecue, from our indulgent and fudgy brownies (page 152) to our light, crispy phyllo pastry custard berry pie (page 155).

These are our family-favorite desserts and we hope they will become your favorites too!

Divine CHOCOLATE FUDGE BROWNIES

YIELD
9 large servings,
18 small servings

Our Divine Chocolate Fudge Brownies are what every chocolate connoisseur's dreams are made of. They're rich and decadent, with just the right amount of fudgy goodness, topped with an exquisite chocolate sauce that you can enjoy hot or cold. We turn our grill into an outside oven by setting it up to cook indirectly, with the lid closed. These brownies are fabulously fudgy and will be a hit at your next barbeque party.

BROWNIES

1 cup (126 g) milk or dark chocolate, chopped

½ cup (114 g) butter, melted

1 cup (200 g) granulated sugar

Pinch of salt

2 eggs

1 tsp vanilla extract

1 cup (125 g) all-purpose flour, sifted

3 tbsp (16 g) cocoa powder

1 cup (168 g) white chocolate chips

CHOCOLATE SAUCE

1¼ cups (175 g) dark chocolate, chopped

1 cup (240 ml) water

¼ cup (60 ml) heavy cream

5 tbsp (75 g) superfine (caster) sugar

1 tsp vanilla extract

2 tsp (10 g) butter

1 tbsp (15 ml) brandy (optional)

Prepare a grill for indirect heat (see the Frequently Asked Grilling Questions section on page 10) and preheat it to 325°F (165°C).

Grease an 8-inch (20-cm) square baking pan then line with parchment paper. The baking pan needs to be able to be used in a grill, so check the manufacturer's instructions. Use a baking rack set in the grill when baking to elevate the pan and help shield the cake from direct heat, which will prevent it from burning.

Using a gas side burner or a stovetop, bring a medium saucepan of water to a simmer and place the milk or dark chocolate in a heatproof bowl. Place the bowl over the simmering water and stir until the chocolate has melted and is smooth. This will take 3 to 5 minutes. Set the bowl aside to cool slightly.

While the chocolate is cooling, in a large bowl, beat the butter and sugar until light and fluffy. Then stir in the salt, eggs and vanilla until well combined. Fold in the flour, cocoa powder, melted chocolate and white chocolate chips, stirring until well combined and then pour the mixture into the baking pan. Place the pan on the grill over the indirect side and close the lid of the grill. Bake the brownies for 25 minutes or until a skewer comes out clean.

Use a gas side burner to make the sauce. In a small saucepan, place the dark chocolate, water, cream, superfine sugar, vanilla, butter and brandy (if using). Cook and stir for 5 minutes or until all the ingredients have melted and the sauce is smooth and has slightly thickened.

Slice and serve the brownies with the Chocolate Sauce.

Creamy CUSTARD BERRY DELICIOUS PIE

YIELD
8–10 slices

We have turned a traditional Greek dessert into a custard berry delight. This dessert is a combination of a creamy warm custard filling with warm, soft, melt-in-the-mouth berries and crunchy and flaky phyllo pastry, finished with a light lemon and cinnamon syrup. This is one popular and dreamy dessert.

SYRUP

1 cup (200 g) granulated sugar

Rind of 1 lemon

2 cups (480 ml) water

2 cinnamon sticks or ½ tsp ground cinnamon

CREAMY CUSTARD

2 tbsp (22 g) fine semolina

2 tbsp (28 g) custard powder (or vanilla pudding mix)

½ cup (64 g) cornstarch

½ cup (120 g) sugar

1 tsp vanilla extract

½ tsp lemon zest

6 cups (1.4 L) whole milk

1 egg yolk

1 cup (227 g) unsalted butter

1 (14-oz [397-g]) package phyllo pastry dough, thawed

1 cup (123 g) fresh raspberries, divided

1 cup (148 g) fresh blueberries, divided

To make the syrup, prepare a gas barbecue or kettle for direct heat and preheat it to 355°F (180°C).

In a small saucepan set on the grill, add the sugar, lemon rind, water and cinnamon stick and give it a gentle stir. When the syrup starts to the boil, lower the heat then simmer until the syrup has slightly thickened, 8 to 10 minutes. Remove the saucepan from the heat and allow it to cool completely.

Meanwhile, to make the custard, in a large saucepan combine the semolina, custard powder, cornstarch, sugar, vanilla and lemon zest. Gradually add the milk while stirring with a whisk so no lumps form. Add the egg yolk and stir vigorously until everything has combined. Place the saucepan on the hot barbecue, stirring constantly until the custard starts to thicken, about 10 minutes. Remove the saucepan from the heat and add a layer of cling wrap to the top of the custard to prevent it from forming a crust. Allow the custard to cool slightly.

Place a small saucepan on the grill and melt the butter. When the butter is melted, using a pastry brush, butter the bottom and sides of a 9 x 13–inch (23 x 33–cm) baking pan.

Place all the sheets of phyllo pastry on a work surface. Cover them with a barely damp tea towel to prevent them from drying out. Brush one sheet of the phyllo pastry with the melted butter, then place it in the base of the pan. Some of the phyllo pastry sheets might hang over the side of the pan; this doesn't matter as you will fold them over onto the custard later. Repeat these steps seven more times then pour the slightly cooled custard into the baking dish.

(continued)

FOR SERVING

¼ cup (25 g) pistachios, roughly chopped

¼ cup (23 g) fresh mint leaves

Use a spoon to smooth out the custard and fold over any phyllo pastry that is hanging over the sides of the tray onto the custard. With the remaining unused phyllo pastry sheets, work with one sheet at a time and brush with butter then carefully scrunch it up to bring long sides together to make a loose rope and place it on top of the custard. Repeat this with the phyllo pastry sheets until all the custard is covered. The more phyllo pastry sheet you have on top of the custard, the crunchier the pie will be. Scatter half of the raspberries and blueberries over the scrunched phyllo. Reserve the other half to add to the pie once it comes off the grill.

Prepare a gas barbecue or kettle for indirect heat (see the Frequently Asked Grilling Questions section on page 10) and preheat it to 355°F (180°C) with the lid closed.

Place the baking pan on a baking rack placed on the indirect grill grate to elevate the tray and help shield the pie from direct heat to prevent it from burning. Cook for 35 to 45 minutes, until golden brown. Take the pie off the barbecue and pour the cold syrup all over. Sprinkle with reserved raspberries and blueberries. Let the pie sit for 15 minutes before slicing.

Serve with the chopped pistachios and mint leaves.

Wicked WALNUT BBQ CAKE

YIELD
6 servings

This Wicked Walnut BBQ Cake never disappoints. It's soft and melts in your mouth with a mild crunch from the walnuts. The cinnamon gives a nice earthy taste and the light syrup gives it a softness that makes this cake irresistible and perfect to cook on the grill. It is a Greek cake our mother would make as we were growing up but with a few changes to the recipe. For a little point of difference, you can also add a few dark chocolate drops when adding the walnuts.

SYRUP

1 cup (200 g) granulated sugar

2 cups (480 ml) water

Rind of 1 lemon

2 cinnamon sticks

¼ tsp ground cinnamon

CAKE

1½ cups (180 g) self-rising flour

2 tsp (9 g) baking powder

1 tsp cinnamon

½ tsp ground nutmeg

¼ tsp ground cloves

¼ tsp salt

9 tbsp (125 g) butter, softened

1½ cups (300 g) sugar

4 eggs

½ tsp vanilla extract

½ cup (120 ml) freshly squeezed orange juice

¼ cup (60 ml) cognac

1 cup (117 g) chopped walnuts

6 walnuts, whole, for garnish

Grease an 8-inch (20-cm) cast-iron skillet, then line it with parchment paper on the base and sides, so the cake will come out easier when it is ready.

Prepare a gas grill for indirect heat (see the Frequently Asked Grilling Questions section on page 10) and preheat it to 365°F (180°C) with the lid down. Place a baking rack on the middle grill to elevate the cake and to help shield it from direct heat to prevent burning.

On the hot side of the grill, prepare the syrup. In a medium-sized pan stir the sugar, water, lemon rind, cinnamon sticks and cinnamon. Bring the mixture to a boil, then reduce the heat to a simmer until the syrup thickens slightly, approximately 10 minutes. Don't let the syrup thicken too much or it will become too sweet.

Meanwhile, in a medium bowl, sift the flour, baking powder, cinnamon, nutmeg, cloves and salt.

In a large bowl, use an electric mixer to cream the butter and sugar until it becomes fluffy and lighter in color. This will take approximately 5 minutes, and it will make the cake nice and light when it is cooked. Continue mixing and beat in the eggs, one at a time, then add the vanilla, orange juice and cognac. Slowly fold in the dry ingredients while continuing to mix until the batter is smooth. Stir in the chopped walnuts.

Pour the batter into the parchment-lined skillet and place it on the grill on the side opposite the flame for indirect cooking for 25 to 30 minutes or until a skewer inserted in the middle of the cake comes out clean.

With a skewer, pierce little holes all over the top of the cake and then use a tablespoon to spoon the syrup all over the cake. The cake will absorb all the syrup.

Serve each slice with a piece of walnut on top.

APPLE CRUMBLE BBQ CAKE

YIELD
9 servings

Everybody loves apple crumble and this cake is irresistible! We find that this recipe is not only a great way to use up some extra apples, but it can bake while you are enjoying an outdoor barbecue lunch or dinner. Although this recipe works well in all barbecues when they're set up for indirect cooking, it can also be baked in an indoor oven. Our families love this recipe and we know you will too.

CRUMBLE TOPPING
½ cup (63 g) all-purpose flour

¼ cup (57 g) cold butter, diced

½ cup (110 g) brown sugar

¼ cup (27 g) chopped pecans (optional)

1 tsp cinnamon

CAKE
1 stick (110 g) butter, melted

1 cup (200 g) sugar

1 egg

1 tsp vanilla extract

2 cups (500 g) all-purpose flour

1 tsp baking powder

½ tsp cinnamon

Pinch of salt

1 cup (240 ml) milk

3 green apples, peeled, cored and sliced

Confectioners' sugar (for dusting)

Maple syrup (optional)

Prepare a grill for indirect heat (see the Frequently Asked Grilling Questions section on page 10) and preheat it to 325°F (165°C). If using an indoor oven, preheat it to 350°F (180°C). Grease and line a 9-inch (23-cm) baking pan with parchment paper. The baking pan needs to be able to be used in a grill, so check the manufacturer's instructions. Place a baking rack in the grill to elevate the pan and help shield the cake from direct heat to prevent it from burning.

To make the crumble, add the flour, butter, brown sugar and pecans (if using) to a small bowl. Using your fingers, rub the butter with the flour and sugar until it resembles breadcrumbs.

To make the cake, in a medium bowl, beat the butter and sugar until creamy. Add the egg and vanilla, continuing to beat until well combined. Fold in the flour, baking powder, cinnamon, salt and milk and stir until the mixture is creamy and well combined.

Spread the mixture in the baking pan then arrange the sliced apples on top. Sprinkle the crumble topping over the apples then sprinkle with the cinnamon.

Bake the cake in the barbecue with the lid closed for 45 minutes, rotating the pan halfway through the cook time. The cake is ready when a skewer inserted in the center comes out clean. Serve the cake dusted with the confectioners' sugar and maple syrup (if using).

Umph Delicious Seafood Rub

Quick & Easy BBQ Sauce

Cheeky Chimichurri Sauce

Ultimate Beef & Lamb Rub

The Rounder Rub

Brilliant Burger Sauce

Must Have Pork & Chicken Rub

Essential
RUBS & SAUCES

Rubs are the essential tools in every barbecue cook's repertoire. We've created seasonings that can be applied to meat, seafood or veggies in advance to infuse flavor into the food you grill. You can even make a quick marinade with our rubs by mixing 1 tablespoon (7 g) of rub with 1 tablespoon (15 ml) of olive oil. Double the batches and keep them handy in your pantry. You'll thank us later!

Our homemade Quick & Easy BBQ Sauce (page 166), Brilliant Burger Sauce (page 167) and the Cheeky Chimichurri Sauce (page 167) are so delicious, and are quick and easy to prepare. You won't want to get store-bought again! All of these recipes can be made ahead of time and stored in your refrigerator for at least 2 weeks.

Ultimate BEEF & LAMB RUB

YIELD

1 cup (165 g)

This rub is great for steaks, roasts and lamb chops, but try it on beef ribs, brisket and burnt ends too. It's packed full of flavor!

3 tbsp (21 g) ground sweet paprika

2 tbsp (14 g) smoked paprika

2 tbsp (36 g) kosher salt

3 tbsp (21 g) onion powder

3 tbsp (24 g) garlic powder

3 tbsp (15 g) dried oregano

2 tbsp (13 g) pepper

2 tbsp (28 g) light brown sugar

2 tbsp (8 g) mustard powder

1 tbsp (6 g) ground cumin

2 tsp (4 g) ground allspice

2 tsp (9 g) celery salt

1 tsp cayenne pepper

In a small bowl, mix the sweet paprika, smoked paprika, salt, onion powder, garlic powder, oregano, pepper, brown sugar, mustard powder, cumin, allspice, celery salt and cayenne pepper. Mix well to combine.

Store in an airtight container for 2 to 3 months.

Must-Have PORK & CHICKEN RUB

YIELD

1 cup (165 g)

The flavor combinations in this rub make it perfect for pulled pork, ribs and all chicken. It's an easy rub to make and one you'll always want on hand.

5 tbsp (35 g) ground sweet paprika

3 tbsp (24 g) ground garlic powder

2 tbsp (14 g) ground onion powder

1 tbsp (7 g) ground turmeric

2 tbsp (12 g) ground mustard powder

1 tbsp (3 g) dried oregano

1 tbsp (3 g) dried thyme

1 tbsp (7 g) ground sage

1 tbsp (5 g) ground ginger

2 tbsp (36 g) salt

1 tbsp (6 g) pepper

In a small bowl, mix the sweet paprika, garlic powder, onion powder, turmeric, mustard powder, oregano, thyme, sage, ginger, salt and pepper. Mix well to combine.

Store in an airtight container for 2 to 3 months.

BBQ COFFEE RUB

YIELD
⅓ cup (42 g)

This rub is perfect for beef and the coffee adds an earthy, yet subtle next-level flavor.

1 tbsp (7 g) finely ground coffee beans

1 tbsp (14 g) brown sugar

1 tbsp (8 g) garlic powder

1 tbsp (7 g) onion powder

2 tsp (4 g) pepper

2 tsp (3 g) ground cumin

2 tsp (3 g) ground cayenne pepper (optional)

In a small bowl, mix the coffee, brown sugar, garlic powder, onion powder, pepper, cumin and cayenne pepper (if using). Mix well to combine.

Store in an airtight container for 2 to 3 months.

Simply Delicious SEAFOOD RUB

YIELD
⅓ cup (42 g)

Elevate your seafood grilling with our easy-to-make rub. You'll love it on all seafood, from whole fish to shellfish! Use it as a dry rub or wet it by mixing 1 teaspoon of rub with 1 tablespoon (15 ml) of olive oil for a delicious marinade.

1 tbsp (7 g) onion powder

1 tbsp (8 g) garlic powder

1 tbsp (7 g) ground sweet paprika

1 tbsp (3 g) dried thyme

1 tbsp (14 g) celery salt

1 tbsp (7 g) ground sage

¼ tsp cracked black pepper

In a small bowl, mix the onion powder, garlic powder, sweet paprika, thyme, celery salt, sage and black pepper. Mix well to combine.

Store in an airtight container for 1 to 2 months.

The ALL-ROUNDER RUB

YIELD
½ cup
(90 g)

This is one of our favorite rubs and we use it on just about everything! We always have this on hand to enhance the flavor on all meat, fish and veggies.

2 tbsp (14 g) onion powder

2 tbsp (17 g) garlic powder

2 tbsp (14 g) sweet paprika

2 tbsp (7 g) dried oregano

2 tbsp (30 g) sea salt

½ tsp pepper

In a small bowl, mix the onion powder, garlic powder, sweet paprika, oregano, sea salt and pepper.

Store in an airtight container for 1 to 2 months.

Quick & Easy BBQ SAUCE

YIELD
1 cup
(240 ml)

This is an easy BBQ sauce to make and it can be enjoyed with all food cooked over fire, from hot and fast to low and slow. No need to buy your BBQ sauce when you can make one from scratch quickly that has the perfect balance of sweet and spice.

4 tbsp (60 ml) olive oil

1 medium onion, finely diced

2 tbsp (30 ml) malt vinegar

2 tbsp (28 g) soft brown sugar

⅔ cup (160 ml) ketchup

2 tbsp (30 ml) Worcestershire sauce

Heat the oil in a small saucepan over low heat. Sauté the onions for 5 minutes until soft, stirring occasionally. Add the malt vinegar, brown sugar, ketchup and Worcestershire sauce and bring to a boil. Reduce the heat to low and simmer for 3 minutes. Remove the pan from the heat and allow the sauce to cool slightly. Pour the sauce into a food processor and blitz until it is smooth.

Store in an airtight container in the refrigerator for 1 to 2 weeks.

Brilliant BURGER SAUCE

YIELD
1¼ cups
(300 ml)

Take your homemade burger to the next level with our Brilliant Burger Sauce. It's easy to make and you'll want to include it in all your burgers. It's perfectly tangy and delicious!

1 cup (240 ml) mayonnaise

2 tbsp (30 ml) yellow mustard

1 tbsp (15 ml) ketchup

1 tbs (15 ml) Worcestershire sauce

1 tbsp (9 g) finely chopped dill pickles

1 tsp onion powder

1 tsp garlic powder

1 tsp Dijon mustard

In a small bowl, whisk the mayonnaise, yellow mustard, ketchup, Worcestershire sauce, pickles, onion powder, garlic powder and Dijon mustard.

Store in an airtight container in the refrigerator for 1 to 2 weeks.

Cheeky CHIMICHURRI SAUCE

YIELD
1¼ cups
(300 ml)

This Argentinian sauce is fresh, tasty and unforgettable drizzled over steak, chicken and seafood.

2 cups (120 g) chopped fresh parsley

¼ cup (50 g) chopped fresh oregano leaves

½ cup (10 g) chopped cilantro

2 jalapeños, seeds removed and roughly chopped

1 cup (240 ml) olive oil

½ cup (120 ml) red wine vinegar

3 cloves garlic

1 lime, juiced

½ tsp salt

½ tsp pepper

In a food processor, pulse the parsley, oregano, cilantro, jalapeños, olive oil, red wine vinegar, garlic, lime juice, salt and pepper until the ingredients are finely chopped.

Store in an airtight container in the refrigerator for up to 4 days

ACKNOWLEDGMENTS

A THANK YOU FROM IRENE SHARP

To our amazing editor Caitlin Dow, our publisher Will Kiester and everyone at Page Street Publishing, thank you for your enormous skill, vision, precision and for believing in us. I will be forever grateful to you for this incredible opportunity to publish a cookbook with my sister.

To my beautiful sister Desi, I couldn't imagine going through this barbecue journey and publishing a cookbook without you. Love you so much! Thank you for being the best big sister and best friend I could ever ask for. We've both worked so hard for this and to see our recipes in print is such an extraordinary achievement. I'm so proud of us.

To my son Jackson, my wish is that this book provides you with hours of enjoyment cooking outdoors and you can pass the recipes down to your own family. Thank you for being the most amazing son, and an awesome helper and taste tester for this book. I love you so much and want you to always remember Walt Disney's quote, "Dreams really can come true: if we have the courage to pursue them."

To my husband, Jamie, thank you for the tremendous support you've shown me in everything I set out to do. You've always encouraged me to pursue my passion for cooking and food photography. Thanks for the many times I bounced ideas off you for the photos in this book and for helping me set up my food photography studio. Love you so much.

To my mother, Virginia, thank you for showing me that with hard work and determination anything is possible. You worked so hard to bring us girls up and instilled a strong work ethic and passion to achieve. As we wrote this book, you kept telling us that we could do it, much the same way you always encouraged us growing up. Thanks for being an incredible mum. I love you so very much. I wish Yiayia were still here with us to see our cookbook.

To my two gorgeous younger sisters, Michelle and Crystal, thank you for the love and support you've always shown and yet again with this book. I hope you enjoy these recipes with your families and they bring back memories of our childhood. Love you both heaps.

To my mother-in-law, Lynette, and father-in-law, Brian, from the very moment I met you both you've cared for me like I was your own and I thank you both very much. Your love and support mean a lot. Brian, your guidance and advice has been invaluable as I have embarked on my food photography journey. Love you both lots.

Many thanks to my extended family and friends for the ongoing love and support you show me. Also, for listening when I spent hours talking about all the recipes Desi and I were including in this book.

Thanking God, too, for his guidance. Without him, our cookbook wouldn't have been possible.

A big thank you to all the people who have supported me on Instagram, Twitter, Facebook and TikTok. Thank you also to all the businesses around the world that have instilled trust in me to represent their brand. You gave me the confidence to share my barbecue journey with the world and this book wouldn't have been possible without you. Thank you for the love, support and inspiration.

Finally, thank YOU! For buying our cookbook! Your support means the absolute world. This book is my lifelong dream come true.

A THANK YOU FROM DESI LONGINIDIS

First and foremost, I would like to thank the brilliant Caitlin Dow and Will Kiester, and everyone at Page Street Publishing, for giving us this incredible opportunity and life-long dream to co-author our very own cookbook and see our dream come to life. Words can never adequately ever express how grateful and happy we are.

Thank you to my gorgeous sister and best friend, Irene. From childhood we have always stuck together through thick and thin. You are always there for me and I am so very blessed to have you. I couldn't imagine going through this incredible cooking journey without you. Our passion for food and cooking has always been exciting and now we have co-authored our very own barbecue cookbook together. We have achieved so much together. Love you sis.

My adorable children, Susannah and Isaac, I love you both so much; you are and always will be my world. I hope that you will both use this book as you are growing up and for your families, creating the recipes with love. Susannah, thank you for all the help you give me with my videos, you are always there to help me without hesitation. Isaac, my true taste tester connoisseur, you always surprise me with how well you know your food flavors. Thank you for always wanting to help. You have both been so sweet telling me how proud you are of me and this cookbook.

(continued)

ACKNOWLEDGMENTS *(continued)*

To my darling husband George, thank you for all your love, support and encouragement. You were the one who inspired me to start my cooking journey on Instagram and follow my dream. You are always my taste test critic and I know however much food I cook you will always be there to eat it. I love you very much.

A very big thank you to our beautiful, loving and inspiring mother, Virginia. Your unconditional love and support for us to strive and achieve in what we believe in has led us to the love for food and cooking. You are the one who always says follow your dream and now our dream has become reality. Our passion for cooking first started in the kitchen at five years old when you would let us cook with you and watch Yiayia cook when you were at work. These are memories that live in us and ones we will never forget. Love you so much, mum.

Thank you to my gorgeous little sisters, Michelle and Crystal, for the love and support they always give us. They were our true taste testers right from the beginning and even when we would cook basic meals, they would always enjoy them. Love you both.

I would like to thank my late in-laws Steve and Suzi. Suzi saw my passion for cooking from the first time I met her and loved how we both had a love for cooking. Food was one way of always bringing the whole family together. I know that they would be very proud. Miss and love them both.

Thank you to my beautiful sister-in-law Lana and family and my brother-in-law Stan for all your love and support that you have always shown me. Love you all.

Thank you to my extended family and friends for all the love and support you've shown me always. You're all amazing.

I would like to thank God with all my heart for making our dream a reality and giving us this incredible blessing.

A very big thank you to all my followers and friends on Instagram, Twitter, Facebook and TikTok. My food journey came to life with all your ongoing support and love for my cooking. You all inspire me every day. Thank you also to the companies and brands I've worked with around the world for your incredible support and faith.

Last, but not least, a very big thank you to YOU! For buying our book. We hope that you love our recipes as much as we do. Thank you from the bottom of our hearts.

ABOUT THE AUTHORS

DESI AND IRENE are grilling enthusiasts, recipe developers, food stylists and photographers who have appeared on Australian television, competing against the best BBQ experts in Australia. They have hosted the World Food Championships in Australia, appeared on BBQ podcasts, attended BBQ charity events, conducted several BBQ courses around Australia and have worked with hundreds of big brands around the world. They are both ambassadors for Australia's biggest BBQ retailer, Barbeques Galore and have had a long-term affiliation with the company.

DESI MARIE LONGINIDIS is one half of the Grill Sisters and founder of the popular Instagram, Twitter, Facebook and TikTok page called Healthy Cook 4 Champions and website www.healthycook4champions.com. She's also involved in the family business, Stan the Man Fitness Academy, where she shares outdoor grilling recipes with its members.

Desi is self-taught and has been cooking since she was young. She cleaned her first fish at age nine and was cooking for large groups as a teenager. Her artistic flair and love of food has led her to creating amazing content and developing recipes, and she is also a passionate food stylist. She lives in Melbourne, Australia, with her husband and two children.

IRENE SHARP is the other half of the Grill Sisters and founder of Come Grill With Me, a popular page on Instagram, Twitter, TikTok and Facebook. She also blogs and shares her BBQ knowledge on her website www.comegrillwithme.com. She's a foodie at heart and creates engaging food content, develops recipes and loves spending time in her photography studio, bringing food to life.

Irene lives in Melbourne, Australia, with her husband and son. She is self-taught and has been cooking her entire life. Her recipes are influenced by her travel around the world and she's very passionate about teaching others her barbecue knowledge, in the hope that it inspires them to cook outdoors and create magic.

INDEX